The Lost Graves of Peenemünde

THE LOST GRAVES OF PEENEMÜNDE

MIKE MCLEOD AND SEAN FEAST

FOREWORD BY
GEORGE DUNN
DFC Lᴅ'H

Published in 2020 by Fighting High Ltd,
www.fightinghigh.com

Copyright © Fighting High Ltd, 2020
Copyright text © Mike McLeod, 2020
Copyright text © Sean Feast, 2020
Copyright text © George Dunn, 2020

British Library Cataloguing-in-Publication data. A CIP
record for this title is available from the British Library.

ISBN – 978-1-9998128-9-8

Designed and typeset in Adobe Minion 10/15pt
by Michael Lindley (www.truthstudio.co.uk.)

Printed and bound by Gomer Press.
Front cover design by Truthstudio Limited

Dedicated to Constance, Wilfred, Joan and Colin Fielden and all those who lived their lives never knowing the truth about the fate of their loved ones.
(Jackie McLeod)

Contents

Note. Documents that appear in the Appendix are referenced in the main narrative of the book as (A1), (A2), (A3) …

Foreword

On the night of 17/18 August 1943, one of the most important raids of the Second World War was carried out by Royal Air Force Bomber Command. A force of 596 heavy bombers attacked the German V-weapons secret research establishment at Peenemünde, situated on the north German Baltic coast.

The crews taking part did so not knowing the real reason for the operation. They were told it was linked to radar, and should be destroyed that night owing to the great danger it posed to our country. We were told that if the initial raid was not successful then the crews would be required to return the following night and, if necessary, on subsequent nights until a satisfactory result was achieved. Realising the reception that would be waiting for them on a return visit, the crews were under no illusion as to what was required.

It was a brilliant moonlit night, with little or no cloud, and a bombing height of 7,000 feet. A spoof raid by a small force of Mosquitoes over Berlin was proving successful and causing problems for the German night fighters, who were under the impression that the 'Big City' was the target. They were having difficulty in locating the Bomber Command main force, but eventually the glow of flames in the direction of Peenemünde alerted the night fighters, by which time, however, the raid was well under way. My crew were in the first wave, having been moved from the last wave owing to a change of wind that affected our aiming point. We were well clear of the target when the night fighters arrived. They caused havoc among the latter waves and by the end of the night forty aircraft failed to return.

On 6 August 2018, due to the kindness of the owner of a private aircraft, I was able to visit the Peenemünde site and was well received by the German authorities. I was also able to lay a wreath at a local cemetery, in memory of those who died on the night of the raid. In the years following the end of the war it was felt only right and proper that every effort should be made to locate crashed aircraft and recover bodies, so that they could be properly laid to rest. In *The Lost Graves of Peenemünde*, authors Sean Feast and Mike McLeod record in detail the work and dedication of the searchers and others involved in such a worthwhile project.

George Dunn, DFC, L d'H
No. 76 Squadron Halifax pilot

Map of Peenemünde published by the Geographical Section, General Staff in 1944, from an older German map (before 1935).

Chapter One

The Passengers

A black Opel saloon journeys through the Pomeranian countryside near the Baltic coast. The driver pulls over to the side of a narrow road and a passenger slowly steps out. He breathes in the familiar salty air of his native land and turns up the collar of his long, woollen coat to protect him from the biting cold. It is December and the temperature is below freezing.

He strikes a lonely and somewhat unremarkable figure, who despite his comparatively young age is already widely respected by his peers and a favourite of Walter Dornberger of the German Army's secretive Ballistics Council. His family is well known throughout the region. His father is a baron and a politician, who until recently had been the Minister for Agriculture. The middle of three sons, the passenger has a determined manner and an intelligent, perhaps even good-looking face. He has inherited his father's flair for organisation and administration. He also has an abiding love for physics and mathematics, and a near-obsession with getting to the moon that has led him to experiment with rockets and liquid motors.

Adolf Hitler, the new Führer of Germany, is sceptical about the passenger and his friends, and what their rockets can achieve. During a visit to Kummers-dorf in October 1933, he saw the first of their Aggregat series of projectiles fail to make it off the ground. That was the A1, and it was top-heavy. The A2 was more successful, blasting off into the leaden skies over Borkum and making it to more than 7,000 feet with none of the stabilising issues of its predecessor. Now they have been given permission to expand their operations and create a dedicated rocket development centre where they can conduct further full-scale trials in secret.

For the site of the new centre, the passenger at once thought of his home as offering the ideal location. Kummersdorf and Borkum are too public, but few venture this far east, and especially to the remote and secluded area around Peenemünde. Stettin, the nearest big city, is still more than 70 miles away and they have a 300-mile water-range along the shores of the Baltic over which they can fire their rockets, and numerous small islands on which they can install the necessary tracking equipment. It is the perfect spot.

The passenger, Dr Wernher von Braun, is eager to make his report.

Approval to build the new rocket research establishment was fast in coming, as was the realisation that rockets could have a powerful military purpose. The land around Peenemünde was purchased in April 1936, and the cost for building the new site was to be shared between the Wehrmacht (the German Army) and the Luftwaffe (its Air Force), at least in the early days, although this uncomfortable alliance did not last particularly long.

A small number of beautiful oak and pine trees that had grown undisturbed for hundreds of years were uprooted from their sandy foundations and cleared to make way for an airfield to the west of the peninsula, an airfield that would later serve its own purpose as a test bed for experimental Luftwaffe aircraft. In the east were the laboratories and workshops to feed the test stands along the eastern shore and to the north. A housing estate, accommodation blocks and other administrative buildings were also constructed to house the small army of scientists, engineers and technicians who would soon arrive, their number later swollen by willing and unwilling workers from the Reich.

Work began as soon as was practicably possible on a new rocket, the A3, with a newly designed motor giving it a 1½-ton thrust. Von Braun calculated that a larger rocket, the A4, was possible, with a 20-ton thrust being capable of carrying a 1-ton heavy explosive payload over a distance of up to 200 miles. While he had once dreamed of sending rockets to the moon, now he thought of war, and von Braun already had half an eye on the rocket's true military potential.

The A3, however, was not a success, and early trials were deeply disappointing. Prototypes crashed prematurely with alarming regularity, and plans for the A4 military rocket were shelved, at least for the time being. Meantime, the Wehrmacht continued to build. Peenemünde soon had its own private power station, its own large liquid oxygen factory, and numerous other secret installations to support its rocket programme.

Field Marshal Walther von Brauchitsch, commander-in-chief of the German Army, ordered a pilot factory to be built to explore the mass production of the yet-unproven A4, and with the outbreak of war, plans for mass-producing the potentially devastating rocket were brought forward to commence in May 1941.

The success of the German military in Poland temporarily put the plans on hold. The ease with which the Germans had secured their early victories convinced Hitler that his rockets were no longer a priority; failure to defeat Britain, however, and the stubborn resistance of the sceptred isle and its Allies, persuaded him to renew his interest, and his patronage, providing the rocket development programme with an 'SS' rating – giving it the highest priority.

The ebb and flow of Germany's fortunes impacted directly on the speed with which the research was conducted and the materials and investment provided. Raw materials, such as steel, and other expensive commodities including manpower, were in great demand, and to some the rocket programme appeared little more than an expensive and fanciful folly. Even Hitler himself once again came to regard the programme with some scepticism until the bombing of Lübeck, when the RAF recorded one of its most successful area bombing raids of the entire war. A huge firestorm caused massive damage to the city centre, destroying three historic churches. The Führer was furious at this attack on German culture, and ordered Dornberger, through the Minister of Munitions Albert Speer, to prepare a feasibility study for the production of 3,000 rockets per month.

His request, however, coincided with a low point in the A4's development. The prototype exploded during a combustion-chamber trial. That was on 18 March 1942. Hitler's demands became more extravagant, obliging Dornberger to gently rein in his leader's expectations. It was not so much the manufacturing process that was the issue, but rather the fuel, and liquid oxygen could not be easily stored. For the moment, though, they didn't even have a rocket that worked.

Testing of the second prototype followed a similar path and failed. This one, at least, managed to make it into the air and beyond 16,000 feet before it fell apart, the sad remains splashing down in the sea only a mile from where it left with such great hope. A third rocket also met with disaster when its internal electric power supply failed. But, promisingly, it had reached 35,000 feet at twice the speed of sound.

On the afternoon of 3 October 1942, after months of frustration and humiliation for the Army men, a crowd of anxious engineers and technicians gathered to watch the fourth prototype lift from Test Stand VII and make its way effortlessly into the sky and rapidly gain height over the Baltic coast. Cameras clicked and a team from Germany's propaganda unit were on hand to capture the event on film. It was a moment of wonder and relief for Dornberger, von Braun and his team, witnessing the 13-ton monster complete its first fully successful flight. Two months later, on Speer's recommendation, the Führer signed a decree for the weapon's mass production. Money and resources that had previously been hard to come by would no longer be limited and searches began for suitable launching sites in northern France. London was to be the target.

While the German Army basked in its new-found popularity, the German Air Force sulked, bemoaning the fact that the Wehrmacht appeared to have 'sprouted wings'. The Army had beaten their Air Force colleagues to the punch, but the Luftwaffe had its own ace in the hole, a small, pilotless aircraft capable of carrying almost one ton of explosive 150 miles.

Initiated by the engine manufacturer Argus, the pilotless plane was powered by a pulse-jet unit that was simple and inexpensive to build and generally reliable. While primitive, it was deemed 'fit for purpose'. Fieseler, the Kassel-based manufacturer whose aircraft were largely powered by Argus engines, designed the airframe, and on Christmas Eve 1942 the first of the new generation of 'flying bomb' was successfully catapulted into the sky. While the Fi.103, as it was officially designated, had not been conceived or designed at Peenemünde, the Luftwaffe airfield was the natural choice for its launch testing.

The flying bomb had many advantages; for one, it was considerably less expensive than its A4 stablemate, and very easy to mass-produce. It was also easy to set up and launch, a factor that was to cause immense frustration to Bomber Command before the invasion of Europe, which was tasked with wiping out the menace. On the downside, the bomb had to fly straight and level, at a fixed height and at a comparatively slow speed, making it a relatively easy target for British anti-aircraft defences.

Despite these shortcomings, the Air Force was back in favour, and the German military now had two viable weapons with which it could launch a sustained attack on the enemy's capital.

By the spring of 1943, A4 rockets were being fired and tested on an almost weekly basis. Work was also well under way on completing the second of two massive workshops, where full production was planned. Whereas the first rockets had been virtually hand-built and assembled on site, future production would be shared across three sites – Peenemünde, the Zeppelin plant at Friedrichshafen, and a third factory at Wiener Neustadt in Austria. Between the three of them, the Germans planned to build some 950 rockets per month by the end of 1943.

With so much activity, the Germans were rightly concerned that not only must their work be discovered, but that an attack on Peenemünde was highly probable. The huge number of foreign workers present made it likely that intelligence was getting back to the British via the resistance, and high-flying photo-reconnaissance aircraft had buzzed the site on more than one occasion, dangerous specks in the sky searching for the unusual. The oaks and pines could conceal a great deal, but the facility had grown to such a size that true camouflage was virtually impossible.

Plans were set in place to safeguard all of the blueprints and special tools, such that a new location could be established quickly should an attack occur and serious damage be inflicted. It was not until the night of 17/18 August 1943, however, that the Germans would be sure that their secret was out.

It is the morning of 16 August 1943. A car with distinctive RAF markings pulls up outside an eighteenth-century country house in the picturesque market town of Huntingdon. Three passengers emerge – an acting group captain, a squadron leader and a flight lieutenant – adjusting their uniforms and donning their service caps before climbing the half-dozen or so grey stone steps to the large front door.

They report to the senior air staff officer (SASO) of HQ No. 8 Group, Pathfinder Force, a popular, moustachioed 35-year-old air commodore of considerable experience. 'Bruin' Boyce greets them warmly and ushers them quickly and discreetly into a room off the hall.

The acting group captain, John Searby, has achieved senior rank in a comparatively short space of time, but then war has a habit of accelerating promotion. He looks every inch the typical RAF hero, with a profile reminiscent of a marble bust from another heroic age. His rank is all the more remarkable given that he was a 'Brat', an aircraft apprentice at Halton before the war. He was also later a sergeant pilot, then singled out for a commission and sent on a Specialist Navigation course (a respected 'Spec' N) – a qualification much in demand. Until recently he'd been a flight commander at No. 106 Squadron, deputising to a young officer commanding by the name of Guy Gibson. He'd expected to go on leave at the end of his tour, but the higher echelons had decided otherwise. It had even been rumoured that Gibson had him earmarked for his own special operation, but it was not to be.

Searby is now the officer commanding No. 83 Squadron, a Pathfinder squadron, flying in the vanguard of all Main Force attacks to identify and mark enemy targets throughout western Europe, including fascist Italy.

With Searby are the two other officers, Squadron Leader Norman Scrivenor and Flight Lieutenant George Ross. The diminutive Scrivenor, a navigator, is thorough and precise, and a recognised expert in his field. He is also unquestionably brave, and by the war's end will have notched up around 100 sorties, many with the Pathfinder Force (PFF). George Ross, an air bomber, has the look of a scholar, with his round glasses and calm, gentle manner. Cool and resolute under pressure, Ross wears the ribbon of the Distinguished Flying Medal (DFM) beneath his half-wing brevet. He too is an expert at his 'trade'.

In the room is another officer, the air officer commanding (AOC) No. 8 Group, Donald Bennett. Bennett, an Australian and expert pilot and navigator in his own right, is not one for small talk, and is standing studying a large, papier mâché model. All eyes are drawn to its size, and details of buildings and what look like factories bordering a long section of coastline. The visitors are not told what the model represents, beyond being an 'experimental station' that they can expect to bomb in the next day or two. Bennett draws their attention to various features and bids that they commit what they see to memory. Still they are not told its location, but the air of secrecy has them transfixed.

Bennett is busy and has other matters to attend but invites the men to stay and study the model and accompanying target photographs more closely. There are three targets extending in a largely straight line north to south. George is examining the model from every angle. It has been well put together from a series of RAF reconnaissance photographs and on-the-ground intelligence. Whereas Searby and Scrivenor will find the target for him, the success of the operation will depend entirely on how accurately the three aiming points are marked.

The visitors have seen enough. They bid their farewells to Boyce, who in turn wishes them luck. Boyce will join them later for the raid, flying incognito with a crew from No. 97 Squadron. It will be a spur of the moment decision, and he hopes his boss, Bennett, doesn't mind.[1]

There is much to discuss. Within twenty-four hours they will learn the name of their target, its location and its purpose. The establishment that Dr Wernher von Braun has spent many years creating in Peenemünde will take less than an hour to destroy.

On the morning of 17 August, the AOC-in-C Bomber Command, Arthur 'Butch' Harris, ordered his deputy, the ever-faithful Robert Saundby, to lay on Operation 'Hydra' and a smaller raid on 'Whitebait' – coordinated attacks on Peenemünde and Berlin. He was satisfied that the weather conditions were favourable. The attack on Peenemünde was the 'main event'; the raid on Berlin, a spoof to draw the German night fighters away from the real intended target.

The AOC No. 8 Group was the first to be informed. Pathfinders were asked to provide ninety-seven aircraft, with a zero-hour of fifteen minutes after midnight. PFF was also responsible for the 'spoof', detailing eight Mosquitoes from No. 139 Squadron. John Searby, officer commanding No. 83 Squadron at Wyton, was told soon afterwards that Harris had ordered a 'Goodwood' – the code for a maximum effort. He was also told that he was to act as 'Master Bomber'.

His selection as Master Bomber had not come as a surprise. A fortnight earlier, Pathfinder Force had trialled a new method of attack over Turin, and it had been an outstanding success. Accuracy of bombing had improved remarkably since the formation of Pathfinder Force in August 1942. Twelve months on and the introduction of the 'Master Bomber' was to take that accuracy to another level, and dramatically cut down on the waste of bombs and effort in Main Force attacks. In simple terms, the Master Bomber was a highly experienced PFF captain responsible for marshalling succeeding waves of bombers over the target. It was his duty to ensure that the attention of bomber crews was drawn to certain features of the attack; he also had complete authority to order other crews to do whatever was necessary to ensure the highest concentration of bombs on the target, perhaps by bombing from a different altitude. Instructions could be issued throughout a raid over radio transmitter (R/T).

As Master Bomber for the planned attack on Peenemünde, Searby would be responsible for not only one but three aiming points chosen to ensure the maximum destruction not just of the facilities but also, controversially, the maximum destruction of human collateral. Aiming Point 'F', the scientists' housing estate, was to be attacked first; the two workshops (Aiming Point 'B') to be attacked second; and 'E', the development works, last. Three waves of bombers would strike over a forty-five-minute period, the aiming points being 'shifted' as the attack progressed and at the Master Bomber's discretion.

Blind Illuminators (i.e. bombers carrying H2S ground-scanning radar sets) would identify the area by dropping yellow Target Indicators in groups to assist the Visual Markers in dropping red Target Indicators on the exact aiming point. Backers-up would maintain the marking by means of green Target Indicators. All three aiming points were in line with a small island, Ruden, some three miles north of Peenemünde. Timed runs from the island would help ensure the accuracy of the attack. Datum line Red Spot Fires were also to be dropped on the northern edge of Ruden to further help confirm the starting point for the attack.

Including the Pathfinder aircraft, the total strike force comprised 596 bombers, a mix of four-engined Avro Lancasters, Handley Page Halifaxes and Short Stirling 'Heavies' taken from Nos 1 Group, 3 Group, 4 Group, 5 Group, 6 Group and 8 Group PFF. Some thirty-seven Main Force squadrons and seven PFF squadrons (including the Mosquito 'spoof') would be operating, one squadron – No. 12 Squadron out of Wickenby – contributing no fewer than twenty-five Lancasters to the raid.

The effort involved in putting on any Main Force raid was immense; organising a raid on a target cloaked in such enormous secrecy made things doubly difficult, not least for the intelligence men, tasked with briefing the crews, and the groundcrews, responsible for fuelling, arming and bombing-up large numbers of aircraft in a comparatively short space of time. While Searby had been informed of the target earlier that morning, the details were much later in coming, and briefings rather hurriedly arranged for later that afternoon.

At Wyton, the usual briefing party and 'trade' specialists (navigation leaders, flight engineer leaders, gunnery leaders, bombing leaders, Met officers, intelligence officers, etc.) were joined by Donald Bennett himself, accompanied by a civilian, Duncan Sandys, and an assistant who had travelled up from London especially. Sandys, the Joint Parliamentary Secretary at the Ministry of Supply, was responsible for all weapons research development and production, and as such had taken a central role in bringing about the intended destruction of Germany's rocket menace. Despite his presence, the target was not identified as a rocket research establishment or anything similar. The Operational Order suggested that the Germans had been investing vital resources into developing new electronic countermeasures to combat the RAF bomber boys. RDF (radio direction finder) – the original name for radar – was one of those technologies mentioned as being manufactured on site. Smashing the facility, and killing the scientists present, would seriously hamper the German Luftwaffe's ability to menace the bomber streams. To the bomber boys, putting Peenemünde out of action would be personal.

While Searby addressed his squadron, around the country concurrent briefings were taking place in similar environments. At RAF Dunholme Lodge, part of No. 5 Group, fourteen crews – nearly 100 men – listened to the officer commanding No. 44 (Rhodesia) Squadron, Wing Commander Robert Bowes, stress the vital importance of that night's operations.[2] Failure to destroy the target would simply mean they would have to go there again until the job was done. The wingco would also be flying that night and defences, they were told, would be heavy; despite a spoof, night fighters were to be expected, so gunners were to be on the constant lookout. It was a prophesy that would have dire consequences for twenty-one of the men present, including the crew of a young Canadian, Reg Harding; three squadron aircraft would fail to return.

At RAF Bottesford, a similar briefing was given to the ten crews of No. 467 Squadron listed on the Battle Order for that evening. If the crews were in any doubt as to the importance of the target, the presence of the AOC No. 5 Group, Sir Ralph Cochrane, to give them a 'pep' talk confirmed that they were in for a tough time. The intelligence man did not pull his punches either, so much so that some of the men – seasoned veterans among them – left the room visibly shaken. A raid in full moon was never popular. Whereas it helped find the target, it also made them highly visible to marauding fighters.

The men were understandably anxious; only forty-eight-hours earlier they had lost their officer commanding, thirty-year-old Wing Commander Cosme Gomm, DSO, DFC, who failed to return with his crew from a night raid on Milan. Gomm had been operational since the very early days of the war, both as a bomber and as a night-fighter pilot, and his loss was keenly felt. Taking his place, temporarily at least, was Squadron Leader 'Ray' Raphael. 'Ray' was the 'A' Flight commander, and one of those who seemed disturbed after the briefing. He had been especially agitated by the mention of fighters and was muttering under his breath. He was right to be concerned, as events would shortly prove.

Chapter Two

The Airmen

Reg Harding had been helping out in a drug store before the war interrupted his otherwise peaceful studies. Born in Kirkland Lake, Ontario, on 9 January 1923 Reg was the son of a Bristol father (also called Reginald) and American mother, Rhoda Beckett. His first brush with death came early, when as a ten-year-old he was knocked down by a car and badly concussed. He'd also suffered from diphtheria. Happily, he recovered from both to become a keen sportsman, enjoying games such as baseball and rugby that reflected his joint heritage.

Volunteering for the Royal Canadian Air Force at the first opportunity, Reg enlisted at North Bay on 27 May 1941, having secured the necessary references from his former school principal at the Collegiate and Vocational Institute and employer. Recommended for pilot training, he completed the first part of his flying training in Canada – initially at Elementary Flying Training School (No. 12 EFTS), mastering the Fleet Finch II, and then Service Flying Training School (No. 5 SFTS in Brantford), flying the twin-engined Avro Anson – before finally arriving in the UK in May 1942.[3]

Refining his flying skills at an Advanced Flying Unit (No. 3 (P) AFU) and rated 'average' (as the vast majority of fledgling pilots were), Reg progressed to No. 25 Operational Training Unit (OTU) at RAF Finningley in September, via a Beam Approach Training course (at No. 1515 BAT), to 'crew-up'. Crewing-up was a wonderfully haphazard affair where the men were all paraded together, often in a hangar, and told to find themselves a crew. Typically, the pilot might try and find himself a navigator and it went from there. By the end of the session, five men had put their lives in one another's respective hands, often with no prior knowledge of the individuals concerned, and choosing each other on instinct and looks, rather than any real insight into their technical abilities. Thus a five-man crew was assembled: pilot, navigator, air bomber (more colloquially referred to as the bomb-aimer), wireless operator and air gunner.

At OTU the crew had the better part of four months to hone their skills and prepare for the 'real thing'. Cross-country navigation exercises, bombing practice, fighter affiliation exercises, etc. were the order of the day, with as much work in the classroom as in the air. The aircraft Reg flew was the Wellington III, a work-horse twin-engined bomber from Vickers powered by two Bristol Hercules engines. Successfully 'graduating' from Course 13, the crew progressed to No. 1660 Conversion Unit (No. 1660 CU) at Swinderby, enabling Reg to fly a four-engined bomber for the first time. Swinderby was home at one time or another to all three British four-engined 'types' – the Stirling, Halifax and Lancaster. It was also from where a further conversion unit, No. 1654 CU, was formed, and with which the crew completed its conversion training, flying from neighbouring RAF Wigsley, just five miles further north.

By the time Reg left No. 1654, the crew had become seven to include a further air gunner and a flight engineer, a comparatively new aircrew 'trade' that had been created to assist the pilot in handling four engines.

Flight engineers were typically (though not exclusively) older men, many drawn from the ranks of experienced groundcrew with existing knowledge of airframes and engines. In peacetime, Thomas 'Tommy' Weston had worked on the buses, so did not fit the usual criteria for the new 'trade', although at thirty-two, he was a good ten years older than his pilot.

Born the week before Christmas in 1911, Tommy was the oldest of three children. Originally living in Prescot, his parents – Thomas Sr and Elizabeth – moved the family to Openshaw, an area of Manchester, where the young Tommy went to Verna Street Central School, one of the largest schools in Lancashire at that time.

A bright, intelligent lad, he showed a keen interest and ability in the sciences, especially physics, though he chose not to follow his father as a wire drawer and became a bus conductor instead. He married Florence Crosby in June 1935, the young couple honeymooning in Blackpool before settling down in south Manchester. A year after being married they were blessed with a baby girl, Barbara, although in the event she proved to be their only child.

Within months of war being declared, Tommy had volunteered, and may have become a pilot had it not been for a failed medical examination that found him to be slightly colour blind. His flair for science led him to become a flight engineer instead, joining the crew at the conversion unit, where the role of the flight engineer came into its own.

Behind the pilot and flight engineer sat the navigator, Leslie Prendergast. Les, like his skipper, was an NCO. Indeed, all seven men, at the completion of their training, held the rank of sergeant, which by then had become the minimum rank for all volunteer aircrew.

Les was born in Caernarvon on 12 June 1921 to parents Harold and Margaret Prendergast (née Margaret Maguire), and grew up in Liverpool. An intelligent boy, after junior and secondary schools (the latter at Allerton Secondary School) he earned a place at the Liverpool Institute High School for Boys, a well-respected grammar school, which he left in 1937 at the age of sixteen.

As a scientific instrument tester, he joined the Royal Air Force Volunteer Reserve (RAFVR) at Padgate and completed his time in the Initial Training Wing (ITW) as part of 'C' Flight, No. 1 Squadron, in Torquay. At ITW, Les had been 'graded', and identified as navigator material. His training then followed the usual route through Air Observers' School (AOS), and he was proud of his observer's half-wing (affectionately referred to as 'the flying arsehole').[4] Reg and Les were close friends and had already formed an important bond.

Joining Les and Reg as one of the essential 'PNB' aircrew (pilot, navigator, bomb-aimer) was twenty-year-old Sergeant Leonard McDermott. Little is known of the air bomber. His parents, Leonard and Grace (née Downing), were from Oxhey (near Watford) in Hertfordshire. As an air bomber, Leonard was not only expected to drop the bombs, but also understand the rudiments of air navigation and how to operate the guns in an emergency, skills he would have learned at a Bombing and Gunnery School. He worked closely with the navigator as a team, the two men also taking further information from their Welsh wireless operator William (Bill) Quance.

Bill Quance was married, and his wife Hilda had given birth to a son, Raymond, in the New Year of 1942. His family were now living in Leicester. As wireless operator, he was the crucial link from the air to the ground, critical to the safe take-off and landing and similarly vital in listening out for changes in windspeeds or weather patterns, or if their aircraft should be recalled. There were many stories of recall messages having been missed, and single bombers proceeding to a target to bomb alone, oblivious to their solitary surroundings. Bill would also be responsible for any 'Darkie' or 'May Day' signals, should they be lost or in immediate need of help.

Defending the aircraft were the two air gunners Stan Shaw and Peter Pynisky. Stan was a year younger than Tommy Weston, and the youngest of six children born in Sutton-in-Ashfield, Nottingham. Sutton-in-Ashfield was then a colliery town, and his father a miner. It was also known for hosiery, and at fourteen Stan left school to become an apprentice to his older brother Victor at Benny Walton's hosiery factory, making stockings.

Married on 5 June 1933 to his bride Elsie, Stan moved jobs in 1936, though remained in the hosiery business with Johnson & Barnes. When war came, he joined the RAFVR, and while waiting for his training to commence he also became part of the Home Guard. Practising rifle drill one day in the parlour, he managed to thrust his bayonet through the ceiling, much to his wife's annoyance and his young daughter's amusement. After basic training in Blackpool, Stan qualified as an air gunner at Air Gunnery School (AGS) and met his pilot at OTU.

Peter Pynisky, meanwhile, was a man with a past and enormous character. He held something in common with Stan and Bill Quance in that he was married, and a bond with Tommy Weston in that his father had also been a wire drawer. Like his skipper, Reg Harding, he was a Canadian.

His unusual surname denoted a cosmopolitan background and upbringing. His parents, Stephan and Pawlina, were in fact White Russians from the Ukraine, and Peter was born in Galicia, which at the time was in Poland. His actual name was Petro Pszenycznyj, simplified to Pynisky after his parents moved to Canada and became naturalised as British subjects in 1934.

A keen sportsman and athlete (he was an especially good footballer and swimmer), Peter also professed an interest in aircraft, and was quick to join the Royal Canadian Air Force (RCAF) in May 1940. Identified for training as a wireless operator air gunner (wop/AG), he conspired to fail the wireless part of his training (at No. 4 Wireless School, Guelph) despite being given extra time and tuition, and was remustered as an air gunner only. Embarking for the UK, he was posted to No. 3 AGS and upon completing his final exams he joined No. 19 OTU in Kinloss, Scotland. Frequently in trouble, Peter was prone to drunkenness and on more than one occasion was punished for being absent without leave.

For a brief period, Peter was detached to No. 10 OTU for anti-submarine patrols out of St Eval, long, boring patrols far out to sea to protect Allied shipping, and it was on one such operational sortie that he was involved in a minor accident. On the night of 14 December 1942, some three and a half hours into the crew's patrol and with the dawn coming, Peter noticed some fabric from the tailplane of their Armstrong Whitworth Whitley V (registered Z9157) flapping in the slip-stream and reported it to his pilot. Concerned that it could be something serious, the pilot decided to head for home, noticing that the controls were becoming increasingly heavy in his hands. Upon landing, they inspected the aircraft to find that the port tailplane outside the rudder fin was entirely stripped of fabric, while one of the metal members was broken. Upon further examination by the engineering officer, he confirmed the extent of the damage and its cause. The aircraft had in fact struck a flag post while taxying out to take off, and the resultant damage to the port tail wheel and elevator had been exacerbated by more than five hours of flying. The pilot was exonerated, and improvements in taxying lanes and methods recommended.

As a crew, the seven men were posted to RAF Waddington, home to No. 44 (Rhodesia) Squadron, on 6 March 1943. Waddington was a large, permanent station that was fully equipped to meet the needs of a modern Bomber Command squadron. Originally a Royal Flying Corps flying training station, Waddington was earmarked for development in the 1930s and opened as a fully fledged bomber base in the early spring of 1937. It had been the operational home for No. 44 Squadron since the outbreak of war, when the unit operated Handley Page Hampdens, the so-called 'flying suitcase'. The squadron got rid of its Hampdens at the end of 1941 when it re-equipped with the Avro Lancaster, thus becoming the first RAF unit to operate the new type.

A proud squadron that could trace its roots back to the First World War when it was established for Home Defence, one of its most notable commanding officers had been a keen and aggressive major, Arthur Harris, who was now the AOC Bomber Command and their ultimate 'boss'. At the time of the Harding crew's arrival, the squadron was commanded by Wing Commander John Nettleton, a South African, who had been awarded the Victoria Cross for leading a daring daylight raid on the MAN engine plant in Augsburg the previous spring.[5]

The crew were given a few days to settle in and get to know their respective flight and section leaders. They were also allowed a few hours of local flying to familiarise themselves with the area before finding themselves on the Battle Order for the first time for a raid on St Nazaire on the night of 22 March. The raid, which was led by Nettleton in the company of one of his flight commanders, Squadron Leader Robert Whitehead, DFC, passed without incident, Reg remarking afterwards that he felt the operation had been a successful one, with plenty of

fires observed between the docks and the centre of the town. Only one pilot –
Flight Sergeant Ken Brown – failed to bomb the target, having been forced back
through engine trouble.[6]

The crew followed their comparatively short (c. five-hour) trip to St Nazaire
with two long hauls (c. eight hours) to Berlin in quick succession on the 27th
and 29th. On both occasions their aircraft (Lancasters ED433 and ED331 respectively) were damaged by flak. On the first, they arrived late over the target, and
simply bombed the largest concentration of fires they could see. While most
agreed that much devastation had been caused, the raid was, in fact, a failure, save
for the destruction of a secret stash of equally secret radio and radar equipment
that had been hit by chance a dozen or so miles away from the intended aiming
point.

On the second, their Lancaster began experiencing trouble with icing two
hours into their journey, 20 miles to the north of Flensburg. The loss of lift
caused the aircraft to steadily lose height, and as the navigator marked off the
Baltic coast they were a good 8–10,000 feet lower than their intended ceiling.
Reg considered dropping their load on Rostock in order to gain height, but in
the end decided to carry on to the target, which they successfully bombed. In
leaving the target area, however, Reg was unable to close the bomb doors, despite
using the hand pump. The doors remained open for a further two and a half
hours before they could be finally closed, allowing Reg to land without further
incident.

Such trials and tribulations were typical of a bomber crew at this time and,
indeed, subsequently. Certainly they faced the danger of enemy action, heavy
flak and large numbers of searchlights working together to find their prey, and
night fighters were particularly feared. Collisions were also a possibility, as was
the threat of being struck by 'friendly' bombs or incendiaries dropped from
above. But they also had to confront the perils posed by the weather, and flying
aircraft that, while cutting edge for their time, were still a far cry from a modern
bomber flown today. Icing, where large clumps of ice would build around the
engines or the leading edge of the wings, could dramatically change an aeroplane's
flying characteristics, and at its most severe the results could be fatal.

The squadron lost one crew from each of the raids on Berlin, both with total
loss of life. April was also busy: the crew flew at least eight sorties in total to
Essen (3 April), Kiel (4 April), Duisburg (8, 9 and 26 April), and Spezia (18 April).
The first attack on Duisburg, Europe's largest inland port, on the 8th was

something of a fiasco, Reg remarking afterwards that they received 'no help from Pathfinder Force'. The weather was so poor and cloud so thick that the attack was disrupted and the marking ineffective. They had better luck the following night, Reg observing several large fires and one 'really big explosion'.

For the raid on La Spezia in Italy, Reg took off shortly after 21.00hrs (in Lancaster W4778) and arrived over the target after a mammoth five-hour flight. The defenders put up an effective smokescreen, obliging the crew to bomb on a timed run, using the southern tip of Palmaria Island as their starting point. Despite the smoke, Reg could still see the glow of fire below, and at one point an enormous sheet of flame rose above the gloom. A considerable amount of damage was done to the docks and harbour installations, as well as the local railway station. Reg landed back at Waddington at 06.25hrs, right at the limit of the Lancaster's endurance.

Another long haul was Stettin, on the Baltic coast, for which in addition to their bomb load they carried Sergeant J.G. McD Olding, a young Canadian, as a 'second dickey' gaining operational experience before being let out with his own crew.[7] Approximately 100 acres in the centre of the town were claimed as destroyed, a large chemical works among the factories set on fire. Reg was forced to take evasive action on his bombing run and did not see where his bomb burst.

For the last operation of the month they flew a 'gardening' sortie to drop mines (known as 'vegetables') on an area with the code-word 'Jasmine', near Travemünde, on the Baltic Sea. They were one of five crews operating that night, and the defences were heavy.

Searchlights were particularly active as they undertook a timed run from Warnemünde to plant their first 'vegetable', the gunners opening fire on the searchlight positions below. Gardening required nerve, since the mines had to be dropped from a low altitude. One of their number, Flying Officer William Rail, was so low that he damaged his starboard wingtip when taking evasive action from the flak; another was hit several times in the rudder and fuselage. A slither of cannon fire also damaged the Perspex in the cockpit of Reg Harding's Lancaster, R5733 P-Peter. Harding thought little of it until they landed and did not in fact report to the sickbay until the following day, when it was discovered he had a gunshot wound to the left leg. The wound needed to be treated, and Reg was taken by ambulance to nearby RAF Hospital Rauceby, a former mental asylum, after which he was given 14-days' leave to recover.

With their skipper out of action, the rest of the crew found themselves flying operations as 'spare bods' with a number of different captains over the weeks that followed.

On 4 May, Bill Quance was poached by Pilot Officer Lawrence Pilgrim for what turned out to be a well-concentrated attack on Dortmund. Eight days later, Bill was once again the wireless op in the Pilgrim crew for a raid on Duisburg that passed without incident.[8] While Pilgrim may have been a 'press-on' type, he was nothing compared to their squadron commander. Quance, McDermott and Shaw all flew with Nettleton to Pilsen on the night of 13 May, a trip Shaw referenced briefly in a letter home to his wife soon after: 'By the way, I am in John Nettleton's crew until Reg comes back. I went with him to Czechoslovakia the other night, it was an easy trip too.'[9] What Stan Shaw didn't mention until later was what he truly felt, that Nettleton was a little too 'gung-ho' for his liking. Happily, he did not have to fly with Nettleton for long.

Pilgrim took Bill and Les with him to Dortmund on 23 May and two nights later Les navigated Pilgrim's Lancaster to Düsseldorf, though his pilot was far from impressed with the marking, describing the operation afterwards as 'a most unsatisfactory trip'. Tommy Weston was also flying that night, as part of Sergeant Gordon Burness's crew, while Stan Shaw took the rear turret in W-Whisky, with Flight Lieutenant John Shorthouse at the controls. Tommy flew a second trip with Burness, a RNZAF pilot, on the night of 27 May to Essen.[10]

The squadron moved down the road to Dunholme Lodge at the end of May, only a few short weeks after the new station had opened as a satellite to RAF Scampton, and were more than a little disconcerted at what they found. The former farm estate now featured hastily constructed administrative buildings and Nissen huts that promised little in the way of the luxury they had grown accustomed to at Waddington, but the men took comfort in the knowledge that the move was only meant to be temporary while the runways at their previous station were tarmacked. They may have felt differently if they'd known they'd never return.[11]

The squadron detailed fourteen aircraft for a return trip to Düsseldorf on the night of 11/12 June; Bill Quance was once again with Lawrence Pilgrim, Tommy Weston with Gordon Burness, and Les Prendergast with another pilot, Pilot Officer Derek Sharp.

Sharp was something of a squadron celebrity. In training out in the US, early in his flying career, he survived a miraculous incident when practising landings with an instructor. At about 500 feet, their aircraft, a Boeing Stearman, hit turbulent air, throwing Derek out of the rear cockpit. He was not properly strapped in. Derek only survived by clinging to the tail fin, and thanks to the skills of his instructor in bringing the aircraft down to land despite the severely restricted use of the elevators. A few days later and Derek was nearly killed a second time when preparing to take off on a practice solo. Just about to push the throttles forward, he heard and felt an enormous 'crump' as another aircraft undershot the airfield and smashed into Derek's upper wing, the propeller and wheels missing his head by mere inches.

Fortunately, the operation to Düsseldorf passed without incident. Sharp considered the raid a success. The next night he went to Bochum with Les Prendergast as his navigator and they had rather more excitement. On their bombing run, and with the air bomber in the nose, an electrical fault prevented the bombs from being released. An attempt was made to replace the fuse in the main fuse box, which succeeded at the second time of asking, allowing all but one of the bombs and a bundle of incendiaries to be jettisoned. To add insult to injury their Lancaster (R5901) was hit by flak, severing the hydraulic pipes and rendering the system unserviceable (u/s).

Reg Harding returned to the squadron in the middle of June, but not as an NCO. During his absence he had also been commissioned, and now sported the thin, single stripe of a pilot officer on his best blue. Reg had initially been turned down for a commission, although a comment from one of his early instructors that he might make officer material given time and further training proved prophetic.

The Harding crew, reunited, flew three trips in the second half of June to Wuppertal, Gelsenkirchen and Cologne. The trip to Wuppertal resulted in significant damage being caused to the city, Reg himself declaring he could see dense columns of black smoke a full sixty miles from the target. The attack on Gelsenkirchen was not such a success, the Pathfinders again being hampered by heavy cloud, and the Oboe-equipped Mosquitoes failing to perform. Derek Sharp and his crew failed to return. They struggled again during the raid on Cologne, though despite the difficulties Main Force executed one of its most devastating attacks of the war. A very well-concentrated attack resulted and, for once, they were not troubled by fighters. Only 28 bombers out of an attacking force of more than 600 were lost. One of those 28 was a Lancaster of No. 44 Squadron, flown by Sergeant Charles Hulbert, shot down most likely on its return leg.

Reg and his crew returned to Cologne at the start of July and were constantly harried by night fighters from the moment they crossed the Dutch coast. 'Boozer', one of their 'secret' defensive aids, which warned when they were being tracked by enemy radar, was 'very active'. They also went to Gelsenkirchen (on the night of the 9th/10th) when they were hit by flak, and Turin three nights later.

Turin was remembered as the stormy night that their mercurial leader and Victoria Cross winner, Wing Commander Nettleton, failed to return, nothing being heard of the men or their aircraft after take-off. The Operations Record Book (ORB) simply lists the crew and their aircraft as lost without trace. Many aircraft battled that night through electrical storms, which had not been forecast, to reach the target, but it was not the weather that did for the CO, neither was it the flak of searchlights that greeted them over the Italian city. Later it would transpire they had been shot down, possibly the victim of a night fighter off the Brest peninsula. Squadron Leader Watson assumed temporary command before the arrival of 29-year-old Wing Commander Edgar Williamson from No. 106 Squadron, until he too was lost on his first trip with the squadron at the end of the month. Watson again took command until the arrival of Wing Commander Robert Bowes.[12]

Flying two more uneventful operations in August, to Mannheim (in the company of a number of friendly aircraft, glimpsed in the evening gloom) and Milan (where one of his fellow pilots described the defences as being so weak 'it was like shooting a sitting bird'), Reg Harding and his crew prepared to take part in Operation 'Hydra', the plan to smash Germany's rocket programme. His official record states that in five months he had carried out twenty-one sorties over enemy territory; Les Prendergast had flown twenty-five, and the rest of the crew somewhere in-between. They were all only a handful short of the required 'thirty' that would have seen them complete their first tour, and a six-month reprieve from operational flying.

Alfred 'Ray' Raphael was the only son of a wealthy businessman who had made his money in the film industry before and after the First World War. Ray's mother was a model, nine years her husband's junior, and the family lived happily in the more expensive part of West London. Apart from a year spent in New York, the young Ray was privately educated at Highgate School, one of the more prestigious of Britain's public schools that dominates Highgate village.

Ray learned to fly as part of the RAFVR, eventually finding his way to No. 75

(NZ) Squadron via No. 11 OTU at Bassingbourn. The squadron was then under the command of Wing Commander Cookson. This was still early in the war when the mainstays of the bomber force comprised Wellingtons, Whitleys and Hampdens, all of which had two engines. At RAF Feltwell, home to No. 75 (NZ) Squadron, they had Wellingtons, each aircraft flown by two pilots. 'New' pilots had to serve their apprenticeships in the second pilot's seat (typically up to ten ops) before being promoted captain of their own aircraft and being allocated their own crew.

Thus it was that Ray went to war on 19 July 1941, as a newly commissioned pilot officer and second pilot to a Kiwi sergeant pilot, Francis Fox.[13] Their target was the docks at Cherbourg, a popular destination at the time to keep the German naval threat at bay. Those summer months also signalled a new directive to dislocate the Germans' transportation system and destroy the morale of the civilian population. Coastal targets were supplemented by raids on Germany's big cities, Essen, Cologne and Berlin.

Ray's first operation in charge of his own aircraft and crew (with Sergeant Harry Machin as second pilot) came on the night of 26 August when fourteen Wellingtons were detailed to attack targets in Cologne and Boulogne. Further trips followed, including a particularly satisfying attack on Ostend, with Ray reporting large fires in and around the dock entrance where his bombs had fallen.[14]

On the night of 20 September, however, it all went spectacularly wrong. It was a difficult night for the squadron, with twelve Wellingtons assigned targets in Berlin and Ostend (Ostend was a 'soft' target given to 'freshman' crews). The weather closed in early and a recall notice was transmitted. Unfortunately, a number of aircraft, including the crew of Wellington T2805 with Ray Raphael at the controls, failed to receive the message and pressed on to the German capital. It proved to be a fatal mistake.

Flak was heavy and intense, and night fighters were on the prowl. Raphael's aircraft was hit and his Canadian observer, Sergeant Robert Craig, was wounded. An aileron and part of the port wing were damaged. Through superb airmanship, Ray managed to fly the battered aircraft home, only to find the east of England covered in a thick blanket of fog. Short on fuel and with few options left open to him, Ray ordered the rest of the crew to bail out, staying with the injured observer as he brought the aircraft down in a field. Despite Ray's best efforts, both pilot and observer were seriously injured in the crash, Craig suffering a fractured skull and succumbing to his wounds the following day.[15]

Ray returned to operations with No. 467 Squadron as 'A' Flight commander in the spring of 1943, via No. 29 OTU at North Luffenham and No. 1660 Conversion Unit at RAF Swinderby. In contrast with his first crew, many of the new faces had considerable operational experience.

Navigator Ron Carter, for example, had already flown a tour of operations in the Middle East with No. 108 Squadron. Ron's father George had served as an officer in the Royal Artillery in the First World War, and afterwards moved to India with his wife, Bridget. Sadly, she suffered a mental breakdown and was institutionalised. George returned to the UK, and met a young Jewish girl, Rose Iris, with whom he had a son, Ronald, born on 8 June 1920. The family later emigrated to Canada, George becoming a 'Mountie' with the Royal Canadian Mounted Police (RCMP).

Ron was studying to become a journalist in Toronto when war broke out, and he enlisted in the RCAF in July 1940. Initially accepted for training as an air gunner, he was subsequently trained as an observer, attaining an 'above average' rating. Embarking for services overseas in April 1941, he was posted to No. 11 OTU in Bassingbourn and thence onwards to the Middle East, eventually flying Wellingtons as part of No. 205 Group in the sweltering heat of the North African sun. He survived nineteen operations, primarily attacking Rommel's supply lines as the war in the desert ebbed and flowed, before returning to the UK upon appointment to a commission.

While 'resting' at No. 29 OTU he flew in one of the first of Bomber Command's showpiece 'thousand bomber' raids before being posted to No. 1660 CU with Ray Raphael and striking an immediate bond.

The wireless operator, Derrick Fielden, also had an eventful tour of operations under his belt from the winter of 1940/41. Born in St Albans on 12 July 1920, his father had similarly served in the Army and latterly worked on the railways. Derrick enjoyed an idyllic and carefree childhood before becoming a member of the RAFVR and being trained while still a teenager as a w/op AG, initially at Penrhos in North Wales.

Joining No. 44 Squadron via No. 14 OTU at RAF Cottesmore, Derrick flew his first operation on 16 October 1940, a long, eight-hour trip to attack the synthetic oil plant and chemical factory at Leuna, near Leipzig. All of the squadron aircraft returned safely, though Derrick's Hampden was damaged in a forced landing. Derrick, his skipper, Pilot Officer Skinner, and the rest of the crew walked away unscathed. A further eight sorties followed, including a trip to Bremen with

Sergeant Ayton, DFM, at the controls when he was again involved in a forced landing, until Derrick was taken off operations and posted to the staff of No. 25 OTU at RAF Finningley. Rated above average for Signals, his role was to help coach novice wireless ops into the ways of an operational squadron.

In March 1942, Derrick was posted to No. 106 Squadron to resume his operational tour, this time in the twin-engined Avro Manchester, the forerunner to its more successful and famous four-engined Lancaster with which the squadron was later equipped. Derrick also took part in the first of the 'thousand bomber' raids to Cologne, flying with Flight Sergeant Geoff Appleyard, a personal friend who would become his regular pilot.

Such was Derrick's seniority and experience within the squadron that he was frequently away, being trained on new technology and techniques, often with Coastal Command. It was while he was on one such temporary attachment that tragedy struck. Flying without him and with a spare bod[16] at the wireless operator's table, the crew were detailed for operations on the night of 26 July 1942. Crossing the English coast there was a sudden and dramatic explosion, and the burning bomber fell from the sky. There were no survivors. A faulty bomb fuse may well have been to blame.[17] The lucky pink apron that Geoff used to wear when flying could not save him.

Derrick completed his tour with another pilot, Sergeant Hamilton, in October 1942, his log book being signed by the squadron CO, Guy Gibson. He was then posted to the staff at North Luffenham, home to No. 29 OTU, for a rest. It was here, at the beginning of 1943, that he started flying with Ray in preparation for a return to operations.

Francis Garrett, the rear gunner, was similarly an experienced airman. Garrett was an Oxfordshire man, born in Clifton, the eldest of five children. His parents were of farming stock, and his father had served in a yeomanry cavalry unit raised from farmers in the county. Garrett had in fact trained as a wop/AG, dividing his training between Yatesbury (wireless school) and Stormy Down, where he learned the art of air gunnery and was rated 'above average'. He completed his training at No. 11 OTU prior to a posting to No. 103 Squadron at Elsham Wolds to begin his first operational tour.

On Francis's first trip (on 28 August), as front gunner in a Wellington skippered by Squadron Leader Ingram, the 'A' Flight commander, they were obliged to turn back and land at Docking.[18] His second trip, to Boulogne, was rather more successful, as was a subsequent trip to Cherbourg, but on returning to Boulogne (on 12 October 1941) their Wellington was hit by flak and the following night they suffered a damaged airscrew on a return from Düsseldorf. An even more frightening experience was when their aircraft caught fire not long after taking off on the night of 31 October, but they landed safely at Donna Nook. They returned to base the next day, the ground crews having patched up the damage.

On this and all later trips, Francis flew with his 'regular' pilot, Sergeant Gosman, but he also had the privilege of flying with the illustrious Group Captain Hugh Constantine, officer commanding RAF Station Elsham Wolds, who went on to become the last wartime AOC of No. 5 Group. He similarly flew with Wing Commander Richard Ryan, OC No. 103 Squadron, who had taken over not long after Garrett's arrival.

On the night of 16 April, Wellington R1344 with the recently promoted Pilot Officer Gosman at the controls crashed on its return from operations to Dortmund. Happily, nobody was hurt.

Like Ron and Derrick, Francis flew in the first of the 'thousand bomber' raids, attacking Cologne and Essen for his 25th and 26th operations respectively. His '30' was competed with a further attack on Essen on the night of 8 June, after which he was similarly 'rested' at No. 29 OTU, although rested is something of a misnomer for he flew yet another 'thousand bomber' trip with a scratch crew on the night of 25 June.[19]

Francis continued as a gunnery instructor until the early spring of 1943 when he was recalled to commence his second tour and arrived at No. 1660 CU soon after. His log book shows that he took his first flight with Ray Raphael on 21 March for Ray's first solo circuits and landings in a Halifax. Their first solo in a Lancaster was more than two weeks later on 8 April, after which they were given their final examinations and posted to RAF Bottesford.[20] Joining them at Bottesford were the three other members of the crew, all NCOs: the flight engineer, air bomber, and mid-upper gunner.

The flight engineer, Vivian Smith, and the air bomber, Frank Grey, lived only a few streets away from one another in Newbridge, Monmouthshire, and were close pals. Vivian was born in December 1915, one of six children to parents Abraham and Margaret, his father having worked for the Unemployment Assistance Board as a clerk. Vivian was a grocer's assistant before the war and volunteered for the RAF in 1941. He was happily married to his sweetheart, Megan Davis.

Frank Grey was similarly from a large family, the youngest of six. His father had been a miner who served in both the Boer War and the First World War, being wounded on three separate occasions. Young Frank was a conscientious student with a love not only for all things technical, but also a great interest in art and poetry.[21]

At Newbridge Grammar School Frank excelled, but an early desire to join the Air Force was curtailed by his mother who influenced her brother into finding Frank a job as an apprentice electrician in the North Celynen mine. Thus Frank found himself in a reserved occupation, and exempt from military service. Notwithstanding his parents' disapproval, Frank cut short his apprenticeship and volunteered for aircrew, receiving his basic training at No. 5 Initial Training Wing (ITW) in January 1942. Recommended for pilot training, he was remustered as an air bomber but still fancied he could keep an aircraft straight and level in an emergency.

Adam Brand, the mid-upper gunner, was a Scot. His father, from Dunfermline, had been a nightwatchman in a distillery and his mother a domestic servant from Alloa. Born on 18 March 1909, Adam was their sixth child and had to suffer the hardship of his father dying young of a cerebral haemorrhage when Adam was still only twelve. At the age of thirty-four, he was very much the old man of the crew. He was also married, although he and his wife Daisy – from Alva in Clackmannanshire – did not have any children of their own. They'd moved south with Adam's work, living in Ruislip before the war in throwing distance of RAF Northolt. In civilian life, Adam had worked for the General Post Office (GPO) as a sorter. It seemed a long way from his latest occupation, defending a Lancaster bomber from beam attack.

The Raphael crew was given little or no time to settle in with their new squadron. A one-hour, air firing exercise on 22 April was all the warm-up they were allowed. Ray Raphael's first operation with his new crew came on the night of 26 April, a Main Force attack on Duisburg, where the Rhine and the Ruhr rivers converged and the Germans had constructed a major inland harbour. The raid was not a success. The crew returned to Duisburg again in May, this time a much more satisfying attack that left a large part of the port area destroyed. This was during the heat of Bomber Command's 'Battle of the Ruhr', a five-month campaign to target the enemy's industrial might and factories in the ironically named 'Happy Valley'. Oboe, a secret blind-bombing device used by high-flying Mosquitoes, came into its own, and with the increasing efficiency and skills of the Pathfinder Force the accuracy of every Main Force attack continued to improve.

Harris could not focus his forces only in the Ruhr, however, as it would have allowed the Germans to concentrate their own flak and night-fighter defences in the area, with potentially devastating consequences. As such, Raphael's log book not only features familiar targets such as Dortmund, Essen, and Gelsenkirchen, but also more distant cities including Pilsen (an attack on the Skoda armaments factory), Genoa (where Francis Garrett, in the rear turret, passed out through lack of oxygen), and Turin (the same raid on which John Nettleton was lost).

Over Dortmund, on the night of 23 May, the crew witnessed the loss of another aircraft, a Wellington, plucked from the night sky in flames. At least one parachute was seen.[22] Raphael noted in his post-raid intelligence report that it 'looked like another night of terror for the hun'. It was an accurate assessment. In what was one of the largest raids mounted by Bomber Command to that point (826 aircraft were despatched), large areas of the town were destroyed, with particular damage to the Hoesch Steelworks. Coming so soon after the attack on the Möhne and Eder Dams, Bomber Command hoped to press home its psychological advantage.

The attack even excited the interests of the press. A journalist from the *Daily Sketch*[23] was on hand to record their impressions, and the men were amused to see their photograph and comments in the newspapers a day or two later, to coincide with Australia Day. Derrick Fielden reported that the fires he had seen that night 'equalled and surpassed any he had seen'.

One of the more noteworthy and unusual raids in which the crew played their part took place in the second half of June and was given the code name Operation 'Bellicose'. Days before the attack, crews had undertaken a series of specialist exercises at the bombing range in Wainfleet, and there was some excitement when asked to draw tropical kit from the stores, including a quantity of pre-war Pith helmets from a bygone age.

Lancasters from No. 467 Squadron were among sixty aircraft tasked with attacking the famous Zeppelin works at Friedrichshafen, on the shores of Lake Constance. The raid was led by Group Captain Slee, in a pseudo 'Master Bomber' role, but after his Lancaster developed engine trouble, probably as the result of flak, his place was taken by his deputy, the OC No. 467 Squadron Cosme Gomm.

The raid was unusual in that the crews did not return to their bases after the attack, but rather flew on to land in Blida, on the North African coast of Algiers, hence the need for Khaki shorts and shirts. It was a move that completely out-foxed the Germans, whose night fighters assembled to attack the returning bombers, and as a result not a single Lancaster was lost. Raphael's Lancaster (ED969) was hit by flak, just aft of the mid-upper gunner's position. The flight lasted nine hours and fifty minutes, right at the very end of the Lancaster's endurance, as well as the endurance of the men.

Three nights later, fifty-two Lancasters from the original force repeated the trick by bombing Spezia in the north of Italy before returning home, again without loss. Very little damage was claimed, which is perhaps not surprising given the somewhat chaotic arrangements in Blida that left Raphael's crew with no bombs and only a handful of flares that they attached with bits of wire to the bomb bay. Raphael later reported: 'Suggest that two or three specialists be sent out in advance if the same sort of thing is to be avoided in the future!' It is not reported whether they followed the lead of other crews by returning to Bottesford with their aircraft loaded with grapes, bananas and other such exotic fruits that war-torn Britain had long ago forgotten existed.

One of the ways of 'blooding' new crews, as mentioned, was for novice pilots to fly with a more experienced captain before being given their own command, and Raphael's crew was joined on at least two occasions by NCO pilots learning their trade. The first was Sergeant Colin Wallace, a New Zealander, for a raid on Essen at the end of May.[24] The second was Australian Flight Sergeant George Messenger, who joined them for an attack on Remscheid. It was a small (only 273 aircraft were despatched) and yet devastatingly effective raid in which more than eighty per cent of the town was destroyed. It was also significant as it marked the true end of the Battle of the Ruhr.

As a flight commander, Ray Raphael had duties beyond operations in support of his commanding officer, helping to select which crews would fly on which operations, and who was due for a rest or a period of leave. This had to be balanced with the needs of No. 5 Group to deliver a maximum effort when it was demanded of them. Raphael was not flying on the night of 15 August when another small force of fewer than 200 Lancasters journeyed once again to the north of Italy to attack Milan, losing seven of their number on the return leg. Among those shot down was Cosme Gomm, who was on his twenty-fourth sortie of his second tour. His aircraft was intercepted over Chuisnes to the west of Courville-sur-Eure and blew up in mid-air, killing all but one of the crew. The only survivor was the flight engineer, twenty-year-old James Lee. He remembered his skipper giving the orders to bail out, and the aircraft exploding. They had been the victim of Oberfeldwebel Josef Bigge of 2./JG2, claiming his sixth victory.

Until then, No. 467 Squadron had only lost fifteen aircraft since the start of May and the time that Raphael and his crew had begun operations. The most serious loss had been that of the 'B' Flight commander, Squadron Leader Don MacKenzie, DFC, killed with his entire crew during an attack on Düsseldorf in June. With his distinctive mop of blond hair, 'Mac' MacKenzie was a popular New Zealander on one of his final sorties of his first tour (some sources quote that he had completed 55 operational flights, and a total of 1,750 flying hours). It was a double tragedy as he had taken with him the recently arrived 'C' Flight commander, 27-year-old Squadron Leader Benjamin Ambrose, RAAF, as well as the gunnery leader, Flight Lieutenant Bob Betts.[25]

The loss of Cosme Gomm was a major blow to the squadron. It was made worse by the loss of a deputy flight commander, Flight Lieutenant John ('Jack') Sullivan, that same night. His Lancaster was hit by a night fighter and almost immediately erupted into flames. The author of the ORB writes that this loss alone would have been 'a bitter pill to swallow'. Sullivan, an Australian, had completed twenty-two trips, and was a popular member of the squadron. Only two of his crew survived.

Gomm's death was also a bitter upset to Ray Raphael personally. The two had become firm friends and held each other in high regard. Under Gomm's leadership the spirit and morale within the squadron had grown significantly, and they had become an efficient fighting force. For the attack on Dortmund in May, for example, No. 467 Squadron managed to despatch twenty-four aircraft, something of a record. Ray Raphael, as the senior flight commander, assumed command of the squadron.

It was a position and a responsibility that he would hold for only forty-eight hours.

Chapter Three

_____

The Raid

It is the late evening of 17 August at RAF Dunholme Lodge. The light has now faded and the airfield is steadily becoming enveloped in darkness. There are a few clouds and a hint of rain to come. Thirteen Lancasters from No. 44 Squadron are winding their way from their dispersal stands to the start of the main runway. Form 700s have been signed to confirm that captains are satisfied with their aircraft and ground crews have cheerily waved them on their way.

Each crew has gone through its painstaking start-up routine, pilot and flight engineer working as a team. Ground flight switch on 'ground', so that you don't exhaust the aircraft battery but use the external battery instead; throttles, set; pitch fully fine and locked; supercharger, medium gear; radiator shutters, automatic; fuel, number two tank selected; and booster pumps on; ignition – number three engine ready to go. Contact number three and the engine suddenly bursts into life.

Taxying a heavy bomber on a narrow perimeter track is a difficult task and requires all of the pilots' concentration. The peri-track is wide enough, but it is not unheard of for a pilot to get bogged down on the grass verge and hold up those behind. There have also been dreadful accidents where one Lancaster has run into the other in front, with fatal consequences for the rear gunner. Fortunately there are no such problems tonight.

Slowly, steadily, noisily they follow one another around the track to where a small, chequered caravan is sited and a huddle of shapeless figures in front of an assortment of station vehicles and discarded bicycles are gathered for a final farewell wave and a muttered 'good luck'. The long grass is temporarily flattened from the wash of the propellers as the pilot moves the throttles forward and the four mighty Merlin engines vibrate and roar.

First to get away is Lancaster W4831 C-Charlie, a workhorse aircraft that has already survived eight months of operations and now has Flight Sergeant Walter Holmes-A-Court at the controls. His hyphenated name betrays a distant nobility, but for now he has a job to do, and soon his aircraft is slowly gathering speed as it accelerates steadily along the runway before at last becoming unstuck and crabbing its way painfully into the inky evening sky. The navigator records the time in his log: 21.29hrs. The same time is recorded against the name of the pilot on a blackboard in the operations room. Another time will be recorded when they land; if they make it home.

Behind him, Pilot Officer Deryck Aldridge skilfully manoeuvres his Lancaster ED611 J-Johnnie to the front of the queue. It's Aldridge's 26th operation and he's in sight of home. Four more operations and his tour is complete, but he knows that complacency has killed many an experienced pilot before him, and he goes through the final checks as though it is his first time. It is 21.33.

Bowes, the wing commander, is next to go in DV155 G-George, a Lanc previously allocated to No. 617 Squadron, and he's followed by Pilot Officer H. Rogers in EE185 K-King, a relatively new aircraft. Flying Officer Lawrence Pilgrim in ED433 V-Victor, Flying Officer Charles Hill in JA703 W-Whisky, and Pilot Officer Robert Campbell in W4935 M-Mother are the next in line. Campbell, a Scotsman from West Lothian, has just been commissioned and has only a handful of operations under his belt.

Reg Harding now guides Lancaster DV202 Z-Zebra on to the runway and waits for the blink of a green light. It's a Mark III, ordered from Metropolitan Vickers in 1941, with the Packard Merlin 28 engines. And she's fast.

Reg shuffles uncomfortably in his seat. Pilots all wear the seat-type parachutes as opposed to the clip-on, chest-type 'chutes worn by the rest of the crew, and they are like sitting on concrete. It's a price worth paying, though. If they have to bail out, he'll need to stay at the controls for as long as he can to give the others enough time to get out.

As Campbell's aircraft disappears ahead of them, Reg opens the throttles against the brakes to check the engines are responding evenly, then throttles back, all the time consciously checking the dials. Everything is as it should be and the flight engineer confirms all is well with an easy 'thumbs up'. He sees the 'green' and with one last check with his crew he releases the brakes and eases the throttles slowly open to allow the Lancaster to gather speed.

Lancasters always veer to port when full power is applied, but Reg is ready for it and corrects the swing with firm use of the rudder. Tommy Weston, the flight engineer, calls out the speed as the aircraft begins to accelerate, his own gloved fingers behind those of his pilot on the throttle levers to ensure they do not slip back at the crucial moment.

More than seven tons of bomber is now travelling at eighty-five miles per hour, almost at take-off speed, and the tail is up. As well as the seven-man crew, the Lancaster is carrying a broad assortment of bombs, including one 4,000-pounder, and 150 x 4-pounder, 12 x 30-pounder, and 16 x 30-pounder incendiaries in small bomb containers (SBCs).

With 3,000rpm and +9 inches of boost on the clock, and an indicated airspeed of a little over 95mph, the Lancaster at last comes unstuck and the skipper calls for undercarriage and flaps to be raised, which causes the nose to dip slightly. Every pilot and crew know that once the Lancaster has reached 120mph, they are comparatively safe. Until that point, an engine fire or sudden loss of boost could spell disaster. Tommy switches off the electric fuel booster pumps, keeping a close eye on the fuel pressure. They are now well clear of the runway and perimeter fence and climbing, inexorably, into the night as below them another Lancaster waits for a 'green', and the scene is repeated. Take off time is logged: 21.40hrs.

The time between the first Lancaster taking off and the last to leave Mother Earth is almost exactly half an hour, and that is assuming no slip-ups along the way. The early crews fly a huge circuit, always on the lookout for other aircraft, and wait to assemble. Collisions are unusual, but not so uncommon that they are not a genuine concern.

After Harding comes Canadian Flight Sergeant 'Chucky' Snell in ED665 L-Leather and then one of the flight commanders, Squadron Leader Robert Watson.[26] He's a Rhodesian and a regular Air Force officer who had served pre-war on the North West Frontier and been present during the catastrophic Quetta earthquake in which many thousands – including dozens of British service personnel – lost their lives. Dunholme Lodge is the polar opposite to the heat and mountains of India.

After Watson comes Sergeant Glen Ransom in JA684 Q-Queenie and Flight Sergeant Reginald Ash in JA700 F-Freddie.[27] Both bombers are from a batch delivered by A.V. Roe a few weeks earlier. Next to take off is another former NCO who has just been commissioned, William Drew. A former Post Office clerk who'd left school at sixteen, John, as he likes to be called, had learned to fly in California, where he'd become pals with Basil Rathbone, the movie star. His Lancaster JA897 H-Howe is recorded as taking off at 22.01. It has less than 100 flying hours in its log.

John Drew is the last to leave. He will never return.

At Bottesford, home of No. 467 Squadron, a similar scene is being played out to a similar timeframe. Ray Raphael, now in charge of the squadron, has calmed down since leaving the briefing room. The afternoon performance by the local ENSA troupe has been only a minor distraction. There is still much about the night's operations that he doesn't like; the route will take them close to several well-known concentrations of night fighters, and in the bright moonlight their Lancasters will be easy to spot should a fighter come close. And then there is the method of attack. The assault will be made in waves, with No. 5 Group squadrons in the third and final wave. On the one hand, it might mean that by then the German defences have been overwhelmed; on the other, they might just be getting into their stride, with the surprise well and truly out of the bag. Despite all of these misgivings, he's been ordered to do a job of work and he will do it to the very best of his ability.

Throughout the afternoon, the groundcrews have been busy, the fitters and riggers fussing attentively like new parents over 'their' machines. Everything – engines, instruments, hydraulic systems – must be on the top line. Nothing must fail. The armourers have had an especially busy time. In the bomb dump they have been labouring to load trolley after trolley with the high explosives demanded of the planners. Most of the aircraft will carry a 4,000lb cylindrical high capacity (HC) 'blockbuster' bomb, more commonly referred to as a 'Cookie', as well as a mix of 1,000lb and 500lb explosives. A few of the later aircraft will also carry incendiaries, packed tightly into containers, the idea being to blast the roofs off the buildings and then set them alight. They can't be used too early in the attack, lest they interfere with the marking.

All of the bombs and incendiaries require careful handling, especially loading heavy ordnance into the bomb bays. Their job is not without considerable risk, and the aircrew know that without the support of their groundcrew colleagues, the squadron would fail to function.

The crews have been briefed and eaten their pre-op meal. Of the 100 or so men taking part in the raid, only a handful are in their thirties. The average age is around twenty-two. Young men in the prime of their lives. Mostly fit, intelligent beings; the RAF has never lowered its standards. It can still afford to pick the best.

In the crew room, the men follow their usual routines and rituals. Personal items are left in the locker. Most have written letters to be sent to their loved one 'in the event of my death'. The admin boys have also seen to it that they have left a will.

Ray is chatting to his navigator, Ron Carter, and clambering on to the crew bus to take them to dispersal where Lancaster LM342 is waiting. It's a Mark III featuring four Packard Merlin 28s and is still comparatively factory fresh. It has only been on the squadron for a few weeks, and Ray was happy to take her as his own after his more regular 'mount' – W4946 – was badly damaged following a raid on 24 July. It carries the squadron Code PO-H 'Howe', a code previously borne by Lancaster W5003, lost during a raid on Hamburg.[28]

Although it is a large aircraft, the cockpit of a Lancaster is rather cramped, especially when the men are in full flying gear. The flying controls are neatly and ergonomically laid out, at least for the standards of the time, although an extra pair of hands is always welcome, especially in an emergency. The aircraft was originally designed for two pilots, but now the second pilot has been replaced, and the control column and rudder bars adjusted accordingly. There is an uncomfortable, fold-down seat for the flight engineer, though many prefer to stand. One has to be something of a contortionist to see the flight engineer's panel if sitting down and facing forwards.

Ray settles himself into his seat as the crew similarly take up their various positions. He tests the intercom, and each member acknowledges his call in turn. Immediately behind the pilot is Ron Carter the navigator, who for most of the flight will be hidden behind a small curtain. Ron needs a light with which to work, but a naked light can be seen for many miles across a darkened sky and it is important that they remain unobserved. Behind the navigator is Derrick Fielden, the wireless operator, and the two are virtually in touching distance. It is important, for Ron and Derrick will work closely together throughout the flight. Weather reports will be transmitted on both the outward and homeward leg, and small changes in windspeed can make big differences in navigation.

For take-off, the bomb-aimer, who normally resides in the nose of the aircraft, stands behind his pilot, or further back, by the rest bunk. There are rules and regulations about things like that, but not all bomb-aimers listen. Some like the thrill of seeing the runway passing below them at 100 miles an hour. Today the cockpit is more crowded than ever, for as well as their regular air bomber, Frank Grey, they also have the squadron bombing leader, 22-year-old Flight Lieutenant Martyn Parry, who has come along for the ride.[29]

Further down the fuselage is the mid-upper gunner, whose swing-style seat seems far from adequate for a long journey, but Adam Brand seldom complains. He stows his parachute safely, and in an emergency will simply drop out of the turret, retrieve his 'chute and make for the exit towards the rear. At the back, of course, is Francis Garrett, the rear gunner – the tail-end Charlie – protecting the bomber from attacks from behind. It's said to be the loneliest position of all, cut off from the rest of the crew save for the occasion crackle on the intercom. But Francis is happy there, and confident that he won't be caught unawares.

As squadron CO, Ray is leading from the front, the first of eleven bombers that No. 467 will be contributing to this night's operation. Quickly that number reduces to ten as the Lancaster of Pilot Officer Gerry Godwin develops a fault, and they are obliged to take the aircraft off the line. It is a frustrating time for the young pilot, and although he is spared the dangers of that night's raid, his reprieve is only temporary. In a few weeks' time he will set out for Kassel on the penultimate trip of his tour and not come back.

Shortly after 21.44hrs, Raphael makes one last check and then releases the brakes. Thirty seconds later he is airborne and climbing out, making height steadily with his revs still at climbing speed. Their take-off time is officially recorded at 21.45. Behind him, Pilot Officer Frank Dixon, DFM, recently commissioned, is similarly running through his final checks. He's flying N-Nancy, a Mark III. It's not his usual aircraft. His Lanc has been playing up, and even though his Aussie pal Des Sullivan would never lend his golf clubs, tennis racket or girlfriend, for some reason he's lent him his plane. Frank waits for a 'green', which blinks at him moments later. ED764 is airborne at 21.46.

One of the flight commanders, Squadron Leader William Lewis, a Volunteer Reserve officer, is the next to go in ED541. His Lancaster has well over 350 hours to its credit already and is living on borrowed time. Lewis, too, is pushing his luck a little but will survive the night and go on to be awarded the DFC two months later.

Lewis is followed by one of the Australian skippers, 'Pluto' Wilson. Flight Sergeant George Tillotson, another Australian in ED949, takes off at 21.50, followed one minute later by Flying Officer Bill Forbes, RAAF. Wilson, Tillotson and Forbes are in for a dangerous night, and may have opted to stay at home if they'd known what the German defences had in store for them.

Four more Lancasters are airborne between 21.53 and 21.57hrs: Pilot Officer John 'Fish' Whiting in Lancaster ED547, another veteran of the skies; Kenneth McIver in ED539; Flight Lieutenant Harry Locke in LM340; and Sergeant Dennis Claxton in ED541. McIver already holds the Distinguished Flying Cross (DFC), awarded to him in April 1942, and will need all of his experience tonight. Harry Locke will make history by being the last of their number to bomb, a full twelve minutes after the raid has officially ended.

Ahead of the Lancasters of Nos 44 and 467 Squadrons is the aircraft of Group Captain Searby, call-sign 'Foretop', who immediately after take-off sets course for the coast of Denmark.

The disposition of German early warning radar is obliging him to fly at very low level across the North Sea, and both pilot and flight engineer keep a watchful eye on the altimeter that suggests a height of less than 200 feet as the cold waters speed beneath them. He will keep this altitude until a few miles short of the enemy coast to keep the element of surprise. Not that the Germans should especially be surprised, that is. All afternoon they have been listening to wireless traffic coming from dozens of RAF stations across the country as pilots and crew test their aircraft ahead of that night's operation. The volume of traffic heard gives the German intelligence men some idea of a heavy raid being planned, but for now they have no idea where, and if given a dozen guesses, Peenemünde is not likely to have made the list.

The weather is comparatively clear, with only a smattering of cloud, and there is a clear moon rising ahead of them. Scrivenor, as lead navigator, is concentrating hard to keep the aircraft both on track and on time, since the success of the attack depends entirely on accuracy: accuracy of intelligence; accuracy of navigation; accuracy of marking; and the accuracy of the Main Force attack. Pathfinders have proved their worth time and time again, but this is the first occasion such a complex attack with three separate aiming points has been tried, and they are understandably keen that it should succeed.

Searby has allowed himself an early arrival over the target. He crosses the Danish Coast at 1,000 feet and sets course for the island of Aero in the Little Belt. From there he will head directly to Rügen Island, situated but a short distance from Peenemünde. Up to now there has been no opposition, and the weather conditions have been perfect. Searby is troubled, however, to see a thin layer of cloud on the final leg, and hopes that the final objective will not be obscured. It would be desperate to have come all this way for nothing. Searby pushes the control column slightly forward and enters into a shallow dive, relieved to find that cloud will not be an issue; they can fly underneath it.

Now Searby is over the northern tip of Usedom Island, where Peenemünde is located, and while their journey out has been largely uneventful, their presence has not gone entirely unnoticed. A few wisps of white smoke can be seen below, drifting into the night sky. The Germans are trying to cover the target area in a blanket of smoke, but it seems too little too late. Now the first flak begins to appear, light guns spitting 20mm and 37mm-calibre shells into the air at an alarming rate of fire.

Searby's Lancaster sweeps across the target area while all eyes that can be spared peer down on to the factory below. The group captain is comparing the accuracy of the model with the actual target, to ensure there are no noteworthy discrepancies that might interfere with the attack. He is five minutes ahead of the other Pathfinder aircraft, who for this night's operations are called 'Ravens'. Main Force are 'Crows'. He wants enough time to have a proper look, but not give the Germans too much time to organise their defences. Searby now heads out to sea to await the start of the first act.

Pathfinder Force is organised into specialist crews, all of whom have different roles to play, depending both on the nature of the attack, and how an attack unfolds. 'Blind' markers will endeavour to identify the target using their H2S ground radar scanning sets to 'see' the geography of the land below and identify the aiming point.[30] If the weather is clear, then 'Visual' marker crews will look to achieve the same objective, but rely on the skills of specialist air bombers. Once a target has been successfully marked, 'supporters' from within PFF will be the first to bomb, as further encouragement for the Main Force to follow and ensure the greatest number of bombs on a target in the shortest possible time.

At all times the Master Bomber continues to issue instructions to Main Force – the 'Crows' – and is on hand to judge the accuracy first of the markers and Target Indicators, and then later of the whole attack. If further TIs are required, or fresh marking is needed, he will whistle up the support of the 'backers-up' or ask for new marking from one of his deputies. In every case it means PFF aircraft are over the target for a prolonged period of time, since their services can be called upon throughout. Not surprisingly, they take more than their fair share of casualties. Being a member of PFF can mean accelerated rank, and therefore a little extra flying pay, but it comes at a high price.

Over Peenemünde, 'Blind' marker Pathfinders drop their first markers on time, but Searby is disheartened to see that they have fallen at least one and a half miles beyond where they should. It seems the 'set' operators in each aircraft have been deceived by what they can 'see' below, and the island of Ruden does not register well on their screens. They drop their TIs on the northern tip of the Peenemünde peninsula instead.

A handful of crews decide to go down lower and try and identify the aiming point visually, but again they are deceived. From the air, the Karlshagen Labour Camp looks similar to the buildings they expect to see at their aiming point, and more TIs are wasted. Into this confusion, however, steps one of the deputies. Wing Commander John White, a flight commander with No. 156 Squadron, is not so easily fooled, and his Yellow TIs fall on the dead centre of the aiming point. Searby is ecstatic, and is quick to add further TIs, supported by a team of five Visual Markers.[31]

The smokescreen that started just as Searby arrived over the target is beginning to take effect, and the Master Bomber does not delay. With aiming point 'F' now accurately marked, the 'supporters' make their attack, closely followed by their Main Force colleagues in the first wave. A heavy concentration of bombs is now falling on the first of the targets, and after a slow start the bombers are quickly getting into their stride. The 4,000lb bombs are capable of creating huge amounts of destruction, and the 'crump' of an exploding bomb can even be heard at 10,000 feet.

The first wave is mainly comprised of Halifax and Stirling aircraft, with a handful of Lancasters. In the space of thirteen minutes, some 227 Main Force aircraft have attacked and are now wheeling away, their navigators working frantically to plot a course home as the next wave of bombers await their chance.

Now the first wave of 'shifters' are setting to work, attacking the workshops (aiming point 'B') on time at Zero + 10 – ten minutes after opening the attack. Again, the first markers are not entirely accurate, and only one of the Pathfinders finds the aiming point with any certainty. The 'backers-up' compound the error by supporting the incorrect markers, but their mistake is quickly seen and rectified by the Master Bomber, and the second wave of 115 Lancasters commence their bombing run.

The attack is going well, and in the next ten minutes, considerable destruction is caused on the workshops below to add to the damage already inflicted on the scientists' accommodation and forced labour camp. Dozens of houses have been flattened, the heavy explosives extracting an equally heavy return, and what isn't knocked down is now afire. Two direct hits take out one of the main manufacturing buildings, and others are also ablaze. As well as the damage to buildings, vital parts of the rocket site's infrastructure have been hit, with railway tracks buckled and torn, sidings demolished and a steam pipe that skirts the foreshore on the eastern side ruptured, hopefully beyond repair. Enormous sandy craters are beginning to appear, ugly pockmarks on once tranquil scenery.

Not every bomber, however, has made it to the target. In common with most Main Force raids, there have been their fair share of unfortunate 'early returns', usually through aircrew sickness or a technical fault. A spluttering engine or a gun turret that is jammed, frozen or otherwise 'u/s' leaves each skipper with a dilemma and a difficult decision to make. To 'press on' and take a chance, or turn back and protect the crew, always in the knowledge that the trip will not count as an 'op' if they do, and they will more than likely incur their squadron commander's displeasure. Nobody wants to be thought of as 'LMF' – lacking in moral fibre – a coward by any other name.

At 10,000 feet, a barrage of heavy flak is reported, but as yet the first and second waves have been largely unmolested, apart from those who have wandered off track and found themselves over areas like Flensburg, Kiel and Aabenraa. Searchlights probe menacingly through the gloom and smoke created both artificially and from the burning buildings below.

Some 150 miles to the south, the Mosquito 'feint' has been an overwhelming success, beyond even the planners' best hopes. The eight aircraft have given the impression that a Main Force raid is under way, and vital minutes are lost to the German defenders as they try to make out what is really going on. Thousands of flak shells are being fired from many dozens of guns, and more than 150 night fighters are searching for an imaginary stream of heavy bombers. Having dropped their bombs, Target Indicators and Window, the Mosquito navigators are now plotting their courses for home, ever alert to the marauding threat of a single-engined enemy fighter on a 'Wilde Sau' operation, eager to extract some slither of revenge. One of the Mosquitoes is hit by flak, and the pilot is obliged to close one of the engines down. It's no matter. A Mosquito can fly quite happily on one. It will just need to be carefully nursed. Another Mosquito suddenly bursts into flames as it is attacked by a night fighter. The pilot, a Texan named

Audrey Cooke, and his Scottish navigator are killed in the resulting crash.[32] When the reckoning is done, and the intelligence reports are filed, the records will show that the spoof has achieved everything it needed to and more.

Over Peenemünde, the last of the three waves is now preparing for the attack. The 180 or so Lancasters and Halifaxes from Nos 5 and 6 Groups are tasked with attacking aiming point 'E', the development works. This time the crews have been told to execute a timed run from Ruden Island, at the end of which the green Target Indicators should be placed. A great plan in theory does not work particularly well in practice, and the bombing is at best sporadic. Navigators are confused by the visual reference points, many of which are now obscured by smoke and clouds, and a cluster of misplaced green TIs that are 2,000 yards or so off target.

First to bomb among the No. 44 Squadron crews is Walter Holmes-A-Court, a Canadian NCO pilot who has only been with the squadron for a few weeks and is now very much in the vanguard of the final wave.[33] Ahead of him he can clearly see the other aiming points burning well, and the navigator logs their attack at 00.36hrs, some six or seven minutes ahead of the briefed time on target. At only 7,000 feet, and in the brilliant moonlight, the skipper has a grandstand seat. He feels the heavy bomber lift as the bombs fall earthwards and just as the bomb doors are closing he senses the aircraft being peppered by light flak. It is no surprise. When you are this low, you can potentially avoid the higher-flying night fighters, and the heavier-calibre guns, but you put yourself well in range of the smaller-calibre weapons.

The German anti-aircraft defences are formidable. They have six batteries of heavy artillery throughout the site – more than thirty guns. The 8.8cm flak gun can fire a shell of approximately 20lb up to 25,000 feet at a rate of twelve rounds per minute. Assuming ideal conditions, and a well-trained crew, that means the Germans are capable of firing off more than 300 rounds every sixty seconds.

As well as the heavy flak based on land, the Germans have also moored a flak ship off the north-east coast. It was originally an old battleship owned by the Dutch and scuttled by the Dutch Navy in 1940. The German Kriegsmarine, however, have salvaged her, and clever engineers in the dockyards at Kiel have rebuilt her as a floating gun platform. The *Undine*, as she is now called, features the heavier-calibre 10.5cm guns. They have a slower rate of fire but can lob a heavier shell higher into the air than their vaunted 8.8cm counterparts, and only require a very near miss to bring an aircraft down. They can also benefit from the latest radar equipment, recently installed.

Given the height that the bombers are flying, however, they are more at risk from the lighter flak, and again the Germans have plenty to call upon. As well as the single-barrelled and multi-barrelled 2cm weapons, they also have the larger-calibre 3.7cm light flak guns, spitting out hundreds of rounds per minute at a velocity of up to 820 metres per second. Much like the flak ship *Undine*, the Germans are not averse to using recycled weaponry; several of the 3.7cm guns installed are of Soviet origin, but do not distinguish between friend or foe.

As Holmes-A-Court turns for home, behind him his squadron commander is about to start his timed run. Wing Commander Bowes is no stranger to difficult targets, but this one appears to be especially well defended and he will need all of his nerve and skill to get them through. A solitary green TI drifts into the bomb-aimer's bombsight, and the sergeant who is lying prone in the nose of the aircraft presses the 'tit'. The bombs fall away and he calls 'bombs gone'. Suddenly there is a shattering sound and a short cry of pain from the bomb-aimer's compartment. The clear-vision panel has been hit, and splinters of flak and Perspex have wounded the unfortunate man in his face. He also has a cut to his hand. He'll need medical attention and fast to stem the bleeding.

Only seconds behind Bowes is Deryck Aldridge, who's had a good run to the target thus far, and who can also clearly see a single green TI up ahead. He bombs and as he clears the target area, he sees another bomber close by and joins in a loose formation. If they are attacked, they will be able to provide mutual support. At least that's the theory. In practice, his new-found friend is almost immediately shot down, and then he too has the uncomfortable sight of tracer appearing over his shoulder and seeming to pass right through their bomber. The rear gunner has seen the danger and returns fire, while the pilot puts that Lancaster into a steep dive. A rattle and bang confirm they have been hit, but as yet the damage is unknown. Aldridge gradually levels out and then begins to climb, maintaining the well-held belief among aircrew that height equals safety. Not a word is spoken, and with his oxygen mask unclipped he smiles a reassuring smile to his flight engineer. The rear gunner then appears at his shoulder to say that both his turret and his guns are u/s, and he can only rotate the turret manually. Aldridge sends him back from whence he came, to make the long and difficult journey rearwards to his lonely outpost.

Aldridge is still climbing when he is attacked again, the aircraft shuddering under the weight of fire. This time he dives and continues to dive, hoping to throw the German fighter off the scent, or convince him he is done for. With his engines screaming and the airframe creaking, it feels as if any moment the aircraft must fall apart, but it doesn't and it holds. The pilot recalls his 'second dickey' when his captain had flown home on the deck virtually all the way, and Aldridge decides to do the same. Most of the starboard side of the Lancaster has been badly shot up, and the starboard outer engine is no longer working. Aldridge feathers it and flies home on three.

Along with Deryck Aldridge, two other No. 44 Squadron aircraft log their bombing times at 00.43hrs. Pilot Officer Rogers is more than satisfied with his timed run and pleased with the devastation he has left behind, seeing his bombs fall clearly in the target area. At 8,000 feet, Squadron Leader Watson is some 2,000 feet above him and similarly content by what he can see. He is not distracted by the red Spot Fire burning vigorously and deceivingly out to sea and confusing some of the crews. He also listens to the clear instructions given by the Master Bomber, as Group Captain Searby continues to circle and orchestrate the attack. Like all of the squadron aircraft that night, as well as their bombs and incendiaries they have also been lobbing out bundles of Window to confuse the German night-fighter controllers, though their ruse has now long-since been discovered.

Sergeant Ransom is also listening to the Master Bomber and reassured by his calm instruction. Although both the smoke and the low hanging cloud are causing issues, he is low enough to observe the markers and happy to see his bombs burst close by. He deems it a very good prang as he heads for home.

Flight Sergeant Ash bombs the centre of four or five green TIs, as directed, and is pleased with the results. He might have done more damage too, had a package of sixteen, 30lb incendiaries not hung up. He tries the usual manoeuvres to shake them loose, but there are many night fighters around and he doesn't fancy hanging about indefinitely. A few weeks previously they'd had a shaky do over Mülheim where they'd also experienced an issue with their bomb release. Even with his trusty, pipe-smoking Glaswegian gunner John 'Spud' Murphy in the rear turret, it doesn't pay to push your luck too far.[34]

Flying Officer Charles Hill bombs at 00.48hrs and can see buildings ablaze and a roof collapsing. He can spot little of the further aiming points because of the smoke. Flying Officer Lawrence Pilgrim has a rather better experience, being clearly able to identify the necessary pinpoints on the run-up to the target and then being able to visually confirm the aiming point. His bombs burst in the middle of a group of buildings, and as the bomb doors close, he knows that they have been hit. He does not know how seriously. It is 00.50.

Two minutes later, Flight Sergeant 'Chucky' Snell identifies a single green TI as being where he expects the aiming point to be, and as he attacks he sees the skeleton framework of a long building start to burn beneath him. As they pass over the development works, they are the last of the No. 44 Squadron aircraft to bomb. It is now 00.52hrs.

In a different part of the sky, George Tillotson is on his timed run. Ahead of him he can clearly see the effects of the earlier bombing, the smoke and fire of burning buildings. He keeps the Lancaster steady as his bomb-aimer directs him over the target, waiting for the green TIs to register through the bombsight. On the press of the 'tit', six 1,000lb general-purpose bombs, two 500lb medium-capacity bombs, and a massive 4,000lb high-capacity 'Cookie' are hurtling towards Mother Earth. Seconds later, a massive explosion is seen, reflecting on the Lancaster in its brilliant colour.

Tillotson doesn't think much of the flak, although a three-gun position on the island of Ruden is putting up a spirited defence with fast and accurate fire. The gunners are skilled at their jobs, and both the aircraft in front and behind are hit. Tillotson is more concerned by the fighters, and now there are many in and around the target area. The Germans are oblivious to their own flak and tear into the attack. They are angry and frustrated at being fooled and keen to exact revenge.

One single-engined German fighter has Lancaster ED949 – Tillotson's aircraft – in its sights, but the young flight sergeant throws the Lancaster into a corkscrew – the standard evasive manoeuvre – and then another until he can be sure that the fighter is lost. ED949 will not be beaten tonight. But she will succumb in the end. She will meet her demise over Berlin at the end of January 1944.

Tillotson and his gunners have done enough, and the frustrated 'Wild Boar' makes off to find an easier target. There are plenty about, and it isn't long before he finds another to occupy his attention.

Bill Forbes, in Lancaster JA902, is heading towards a group of five green TIs, but the target is almost entirely obscured by columns of smoke. On the run-in he has been attacked several times by night fighters but somehow he has got through and is now concentrating on the target ahead. His bomb load includes some 30lb and 4lb incendiaries, and as they explode the rear gunner reports that a row of four buildings are in flames. Further large explosions are seen, and Forbes's thoughts return to the briefing hours earlier. He thinks they won't need to be coming back.[35]

'Fish' Whiting has had a relatively quiet trip until now, although the night sky has been alarmingly bright on the way out and it was disconcerting to see so many bombers jinking for position in the stream, their ghostly outlines dancing in the light grey of the sky. Running in from the western end of the Baltic, the bomb-aimer is helping the navigator obtain an accurate fix, and they turn at the little island of Bornholm. The clear skies are now giving way to cloud, and for a moment it looks as if they may have to bomb blind. Then the skipper sees a break in the clouds and below them the Target Indicators. He takes them in, and the bomb-aimer completes his work. They are both happy with the bombing run, and the skipper turns sharply to starboard on a north-westerly course and reminds the gunners to be on their guard.

A huge explosion and flash in the night sky convinces 'Fish' that the Germans are firing their 'scarecrows', some sort of secret weapon that can vaporise a bomber and its crew in less than a second. After the war he, like many others, will be surprised to learn that no such secret weapons existed; the Germans are indeed trialling a secret weapon that night – an upward-firing machine gun installation they call 'Schräge Musik' – but a 'scarecrow' is a fantasy.

Kenneth McIver can see buildings burning below, despite the smoke and the confusion of battle. The bombing appears well concentrated, and his Cookie and incendiaries add to the destruction. At 8,000 feet he is exposed to light as well as heavy flak, and it seems to be very accurate. He observes at least two aircraft going down and thinks of the desperate struggle of the men as they try to escape their burning bombers. Those who are still alive that is. A Lancaster may seem like an enormous aircraft on the ground, but the fuselage is narrow and packed with equipment and other unintentional hazards that make bailing out a near impossibility. The crews practise and practise for such an eventuality, so much so that they can do it blindfolded. But in the air, with the aircraft spinning, out of control and on fire, and with the life-giving liquids of man and machine spilling on to the floor, it is a miracle if even one man makes it out alive.

'Pluto' Wilson logs his time on target at 00.54hrs. He's a good 2,000 feet lower than many of the others in the final wave, and being so low he can clearly see the aiming point and a row of buildings that have already been gutted by fire.

Moments after leaving the target, the rear gunner, Paddy Barry, catches a fleeting glimpse of a night fighter as it sneaks up from below and behind and both parties open fire. Travelling at more than 2,500 feet per second, Paddy's .303 rounds describe a fiery arc towards the exposed underbelly of the fighter just as the fighter's own lethal machine gun and cannon shells tear into the rear turret, scything through the soft metal skin and finding their mark. Paddy has been hit, a painful wound to his heel, and his turret no longer moves. There is much noise and confusion as severed hydraulic lines begin spewing their contents into the rear fuselage, and cartridges in the ammunition runs that feed the rear and mid-upper turrets are popping and exploding. Then, inevitably, there is fire, and Paddy is trapped. He tries desperately at first to free himself, but the turret will not budge, and the doors are too damaged to open. Panic soon takes over but just as quickly dissolves into calm as he awaits death.

Now the Lancaster is in a steep dive and Wilson is fighting to regain control of the stricken bomber. The fighter has gone but the damage is done. George Oliver in the mid-upper turret has managed to fire off several bursts and continues to shoot as he sees the fighter erupt in flames. But by now the heat from the fire in the fuselage cannot be ignored, and he drops out of his turret to retrieve his 'chute. He looks aft at the blaze and knows that his companion is trapped somewhere through the smoke but there is nothing he can do to save him. He's probably dead anyway.

Clumsily, Oliver makes his way forward, intent on bailing out of what he thinks must be a doomed aircraft. He can actually see the cold waters of the Baltic below him and for the briefest of moments a thought crosses his mind. He cannot swim. Still he is determined to survive, and as he comes to the wireless operator's position, he urges his friend forward, pointing urgently to the rear, and the fire. Now the navigator, too, thinks that it's time to go and soon there are five men in the crowded cockpit, just waiting for the word from their skipper to jump. But Wilson has other ideas; he now has control of the aircraft, and on being told of the fire coolly orders them aft to tackle the flames. The force of his language leaves the men in no doubt of his determination to survive.

In the rear of the aircraft the men are now fighting the fire with extinguishers and anything else that comes to hand, and pretty soon both men and equipment are exhausted. Now they can turn their attentions to the rear turret, and their wounded gunner, and begin hacking at the door with the emergency axe. Several minutes of smashing and chopping at the rear doors finally works, and they are able to haul Paddy from his seat and into the fuselage. They are surprised and relieved to find he is still alive and pull him forwards on to the rest bed where they can tend his wounds. There is a considerable amount of blood, and Paddy is drifting in and out of consciousness with the pain. He is aware, however, of their constant attention and reassurances. They will make it home.

Squadron Leader Lewis in Lancaster LM338 is only a minute or so behind 'Pluto' Wilson in the attack, and while he can see the TIs, he can view little else below other than exploding bombs. As well as the flight engineer, Lewis also has another pilot with him for the raid, a 'second dickey'. They can both make out some of the buildings at aiming point 'B', however, and they appear to be completely destroyed.

Lewis drops his own bombs satisfactorily and heads for home, followed seconds later by Sergeant Claxton in ED541. He bombs the centre of the green TIs from only 7,000 feet, and from that height can easily see his bombs as they explode. With night fighters now very much in evidence, he does not hang around for long.

Dennis Claxton's attack is recorded at 00.57hrs. A few minutes later, another No. 467 Squadron Lancaster is attacked silently and from below. The gunners in Frank Dixon's 'borrowed' Lanc do not see the night fighter until after they have been hit and their wireless operator killed, but by then it is too late. The port wing is ablaze. Frank cannot keep control of the aircraft for long and orders the crew to bail out. When satisfied that everyone is out, Frank takes his own leap into the dark.

John Searby, Master Bomber, made his seventh and final run over the target nine minutes earlier, and has now left the scene, but not before congratulating his 'Ravens' and 'Crows' and signing off.

Frustrated by the lack of visibility and concerned by the arrival of the night fighters in force, Searby's work for the night is done. He is confident that the raid has been a complete success – tremendous fires are sweeping the entire area – but time will tell. He is not sure if the last wave was as accurate as the first two, and for good reason. Actually, the first TIs to fall on the final aiming point had been somewhat wide of the mark, drifting 2,000 yards or more from where they were meant to be. It was only some time later that another load of greens was dropped, bang into the heart of the development works. They will need to study the bombing photographs and compile various intelligence reports before they can know for certain whether they will be coming back tomorrow to finish the job.

Searby's night is not yet over. Now at the back of a long stream snaking its way home towards the Danish coast, he is disconcerted to see frequent fires glowing in the night sky and the occasional explosion as yet another bomber falls victim to a night fighter or flak. His rear gunner, Ivor 'Paddy' Preece, spots a night fighter moving in to attack and shouts a warning. Paddy has flown the equivalent of two tours already and holds the Conspicuous Gallantry Medal (CGM), so is a cool man under pressure. He'll need every minute of that experience if they are to survive the night in one piece.

Searby heaves the Lancaster into a sharp turn to starboard and hears the rattle of machine guns as his gunners open fire. He hauls on the controls again and sees red tracer flash past. For a moment, the danger has passed, but Searby knows that the fighter is still out there. And then it comes again, this time on the starboard quarter, spotted by the mid-upper, John Coley. He is also a highly experienced air gunner. Searby pulls the Lancaster into a smart turn towards the attacking fighter as both mid-upper and rear gunner open fire in symphony. Coley puts in a long deflection burst and thinks he's hit it. Certainly, the enemy fighter is in flames but they do not wait around to make sure of the kill. Searby says 'good show'.

Other combats are taking place. At first a small red dot appears on the side of an aircraft. Then, like a burning match, the initial spark turns into flame and within moments the aircraft is ablaze, the light from the fire illuminating the bomber completely in the dark such that its code and squadron markings are visible. Most of these attacked appear to be taking place at around 10,000 feet so Searby drops down to sea level in the hope of avoiding further trouble. The only danger now will come from the light flak installations dotted along the coast. He'll take his chances.

Searby knows that his men are tired, but now they must use every ounce of their energy left in looking for danger. The Danish coast passes swiftly below them and Searby calls for climbing power. His flight engineer moves throttle and pitch control forward and the Lancaster responds like a thoroughbred. Light of its bombs and fuel, she handles like a fighter. Now the North Sea is below them as they complete the final leg of their journey over water. The danger has not yet passed, but it gets less with every mile they fly closer to home. Sharp eyes continue to scan the sky and the sea below. It would be bad luck now to run into a ship, friendly or otherwise, with trigger-happy gunners.

Now, at last, after seven and a half hours in the air, they pick up the flashing beacon of Wyton. Home.

At Dunholme Lodge, the first of the returning bombers lands just before four o'clock in the morning. Squadron Leader Robert Watson and his crew are exhausted, the pilot especially for it takes considerable physical effort to fly a Lancaster. His face itches from the rubber lining of his oxygen mask that has stuck and left a temporary scar, describing its shape. They are mentally as well as physically tired, and the flight engineer is partly deaf from being so close to the engines for so long. But they are also elated. Fatigue is balanced by the sense of relief from being alive, and the knowledge that they have smashed the target good and proper. They await transport to take them back to the crew room and interrogation.

A similar scene is being repeated at Bottesford. Kenneth McIver is the first back and is delighted to have made it home in one piece. The post-op debrief follows the usual pattern, and familiar questions – questions about the effectiveness of their bombing; fighter, flak and searchlight defences over the target; the weather conditions en route and on return; the performance of their navigational aids. McIver tells the intelligence officer (IO) that the heavy flak was very accurate, and they'd witnessed numerous bomber/night-fighter combats all of the way back to the Danish coast. Yes, they'd seen several aircraft shot down, two by flak, one over the target. They'd also seen a number of fires burning on the ground, and assumed that some, at least, could have been burning aircraft. Tonight, McIver can return to his quarters for a well-earned sleep, if he can. There will be other targets and other battles to fight. He will eventually lose one six weeks later, coming down in the sea off Beachy Head on his way back from Munich.

Only one member of his crew survives.

At a separate table, the crew of Flight Sergeant Tillotson gathers around another member of the intelligence team. Some of the men are smoking; others enjoying hot, sweet tea with a tot of rum. They are tired and want their 'operational egg' before retiring for bed. The IO needs to get the information down while it's still fresh in their minds. Did they see any dummies or decoys? How effective was the enemy smokescreen? Was the target marking accurate and the Master Bomber clear in his instructions? The best intelligence men were those who were aircrew themselves or, even better, those who had flown operations.

They knew they had to work fast and accurately. It was unforgivable to appear bored or disinterested. It was even more unforgivable to get a crew out of bed later in the morning to check a map reference or observation that they'd failed to record accurately at the time.

Tillotson says that he hadn't heard the Master Bomber and that they'd been untroubled by flak. He had seen two aircraft hit, however, and had a close shave themselves when a night-fighter was spotted but never in range to open fire.[36]

Each of the crews from No. 467 Squadron has a slightly different take on that night's operation; some describe the flak as heavy; some as non-existent. Some heard the Master Bomber; others did not. All are agreed, however, that the night-fighters appeared to be having a field day; Pilot Officer 'Fish' Whiting describes it without a hint of humour or irony as an 'outing'.

One of the last to be interrogated is the crew of Lancaster LM340. Flight Lieutenant Harry Locke has had an eventful night. He reports that no Pathfinder markers were visible but that's not unexpected. He didn't make his bombing run until twenty minutes after the Master Bomber had left the scene, and in the event as the last Main Force aircraft over the target.

Back at Dunholme Lodge, the final aircraft to land is the Lancaster flown by Deryck Aldridge, just before five in the morning. It's hardly a surprise for the aircraft has been badly shot up, and they've had to return on three engines. He's flown all of the way across Denmark at only a few hundred feet, with his ASI registering 230mph. He was lucky to get away with it, and he knows it. The erks will be busy later today, when the crews have gone to bed, assessing the damage and entering the work in their 'snag' book. It won't be the only entry they make. The wingco's kite is also damaged, and there are tell-tale signs of light flak damage to the fuselage of C-Charlie and bomb doors of V-Victor.

Thirteen aircraft from No. 44 Squadron went out and, so far, all but three have returned. With the bomb and fuel loads on board, their Lancs could nominally stay in the air for upwards of nine hours, but that was assuming constant speed and fuel consumption, and did not take into account the increased fuel used if attacked and obliged to perform evasive manoeuvres, or potential damage to the aircraft or engines. The intelligence officer checks with the watchkeeper to see if one of their number may have landed at another station. It happens all the time. His enquiries draw a negative response. On the 'ops' board, the IO reluctantly marks three aircraft as overdue: M-Mother, flown by the recently commissioned former NCO Robert Campbell; H-Howe captained by Pilot

Officer John Drew; and Z-Zebra, the Lancaster of Pilot Officer Reg Harding.

At Bottesford, the IO is undertaking a similar task. The telephone in the briefing room has remained steadfastly and depressingly silent. There are no calls to relieve the shock that their temporary commanding officer, Squadron Leader Raphael, has failed to return. It is a double blow because he was carrying the squadron bombing leader, Flight Lieutenant Parry. A gloom descends upon the squadron, made worse by news that a second aircraft is overdue, that of Pilot Officer Frank Dixon, DFM. Dixon's flown more than twenty ops, including a punishing trip back from Italy on two engines and a troublesome trip to the Ruhr when his flight engineer was wounded. Now it seems he has pushed his luck too far.

As the hours pass and no further news is forthcoming, the first of the telegrams is dictated for the next of kin. All will use the same form of words, slightly adapted: *'Regret to inform you that your son/husband is missing as a result of air operations on 18 August 1943 stop. Letter follows stop. Any further information received will be immediately communicated to you stop. Pending receipt of written notification from the Air Ministry, no information should be given to the press.'* Each of the telegrams is marked 'priority' and sent from the officer commanding the appropriate squadron.

Meanwhile, the intelligence officers have been reviewing the squadron bombing photographs taken by the cameras installed in every aircraft and operated as the bombs are released. Any photographs that can be accurately plotted are immediately passed to group, and any crews with an aiming point photograph will be given a copy, with the operational details removed for security reasons.[37] The crew of 'Pluto' Wilson will receive one such photograph and a great deal more besides. George Oliver, the mid-upper gunner is awarded an immediate Conspicuous Gallantry Medal (CGM), second only to the Victoria Cross in order of importance, for bravery under fire. His skipper, 'Pluto' Wilson, receives an immediate DFC. After two more operations the crew complete their first tour, though with a spare bod in the rear turret. Paddy never returns to operations. On landing he is taken first to the sick bay and then Rauceby. A few weeks later he is transferred south and operated on at the famous burns and plastic surgery unit at East Grinstead, entering into the ranks of the Guinea Pig Club.

The No. 467 Squadron adjutant writes up the day's events in the Operations Record Book:

Another big blow for the squadron. Our acting CO, Squadron Leader
Raphael DFC and Pilot Officer Dixon DFM are both missing. This right
on top of the loss of Wing Commander Gomm and Flight Lieutenant
Sullivan is a tremendous shock. Like Wing Commander Gomm, Squadron
Leader Raphael was an extremely popular member of the squadron and he
helped no end to keep our spirits going. This was Squadron Leader
Raphael's 19th trip while Pilot Officer Dixon was on his 21st; Pilot Officer
Dixon was recently commissioned and he had completed some fine work
with this squadron. Both these experienced crews will be hard to replace.
With the Squadron Leader was Flight Lieutenant Parry, our Bombing
Leader, and Flying Officer Carter DFC (a Canadian), also two very
popular members.

Today was ENSA day and as usual it was a grand show, a capacity house
being more than satisfied with a really first-class performance.

A similar though less personal entry is recorded by the adjutant at No. 44
Squadron: 'Fourteen aircraft were detailed to carry out an attack on Peenemünde.
One aircraft was subsequently cancelled. Three aircraft failed to return from this
operation. No messages or signals were received. All pilots reported that the operation
seemed to be successful, although it was difficult to form an opinion due to the thick
smoke which obscured the target.'

It appears to have been a successful night overall, and the AOC-in-C Bomber
Command seems pleased with the results. He can't know for certain what damage
has been done or whether he has succeeded in knocking back the Nazis' plans
for a terror campaign. He doesn't know how much of the facility he has destroyed
or how many vital scientists and support staff he has killed, but he does know
that his boys have done everything that was asked of them. He will not be sending
them back tomorrow.

In Germany, there is panic and anger. Phones have been ringing all morning
as the story of the night's events unfold, and the scale of the Luftwaffe's failure
becomes clear. Göring has created a terrible scene and it is all too much for the
Chief of Air Staff, Generaloberst Hans Jeschonnek. He writes a brief note to say
that he cannot work with the Reichsmarschall any longer, then takes out his
pistol and shoots himself. One more casualty to add to the list.

The bomber boys could not have done any more, but it has come at a cost.
Forty bombers have been shot down – twenty-three Lancasters, fifteen Halifaxes

and two Stirlings. It represents 6.7 per cent of the attacking force – at this stage in the war losses are expressed in percentages – and the figure is considered 'acceptable'. Had it not been for the success of the 'spoof' the death toll could have been much greater. The total of aircraft lost, of course, does not tell the whole story, for a further thirty-five aircraft have been damaged. Most of the casualties were suffered by the last wave of the attack, by which time the German defenders had realised their mistake and arrived in force.

The telegrams sent to the next of kin of those missing will be followed by a personal letter from the commanding officer expressing his own sympathy at their loss, and the hope that they might yet be alive and reported as prisoners of war.

For some, that hope will be realised. For others, their loved ones will never return.

Chapter Four

The Missing

By midday on 18 August, by which time it was clear that Lancaster LM342 would not be returning, a secret telegram was sent to the Air Ministry's casualty section at Kingsway, copied to RAF Records in Gloucestershire (RAF Innsworth), HQ Bomber Command, No. 5 Group, and the headquarters of the Royal Canadian Air Force.

The telegram is divided into ten sections A–K (the letter I is not used), with 'A' being the Lancaster's type, (i.e. Mark I, Mark II, Mark III etc.), and serial code through to 'K' being the acknowledgement that the next of kin have/have not been informed. The casualties, and their respective service numbers, are listed under 'D' and in the case of LM342 are:

68155 F/Lt (A/S/L) Ray Raphael – Pilot
980905 Sgt Vivian Smith – F/Eng
J15862 F/O Ron Carter – Navigator
1317456 Sgt Frank Grey – A/Bomb
751496 F/Sgt Derrick Fielden – WO/AG
1353125 Sgt Adam Brand – A/G
1154625 F/Sgt Francis Garrett – A/G
126019 F/O (A/F/L) Martyn Parry – A/Bomb

The cause of their loss is given under section 'G' – presumed enemy action.

In addition to the telegram, a letter was sent confirming the earlier communication with some additional information, including the primary target. Similar letters and telegrams were sent to the Air Ministry regarding every other aircraft

lost that night, including one for Lancaster DV202. (A1) Section 'D' lists the crew
as being:

J.17338 P/O Reginald Clifford Harding (Can) – Pilot
1379790 Sgt Thomas Neville Weston – F/Eng
1127532 T/F/Sgt Leslie Prendergast – Nav
18002253 T/Sgt Leonard Frank McDermott – A/Bomb
1213933 T/Sgt William Henry Quance – WO/AG
1576142 T/F/Sgt Stanley Shaw – ACH/AG
R.104462 T/F/Sgt Peter Pynisky (Can) – ACH/AG

(The 'J' in front of the service number denotes a Canadian officer; an 'R' denotes
a non-commissioned man.)

Crucially, the telegram regarding DV202 includes considerably more technical
information regarding the aircraft, including full details of the serial numbers
of its four Merlin engines to help identify the aircraft – or what remained of the
aircraft – should it be found after the war. The confirmation letter also differed
slightly from the one sent regarding LM342 and includes details of the operational experience of both the pilot (credited with twenty-one ops comprising
a little over 137 hours of operational flying time) and navigator (credited with
twenty-five ops comprising more than 155 flying hours). It is interesting to note
that a tour of operations in Bomber Command at that time amounted to 'not
more than thirty trips', and that this total had originally been calculated on the
basis of 200 operational hours.

The Air Ministry Casualty Section had undergone significant change since
the beginning of the war, a change that had been largely forced upon it by the
sheer volume of men killed in action. It became one of the first public sector
organisations to adopt an 'open door' policy to members of the general public,
and especially the relatives of missing men.

On receipt of the notification of the failure of an aircraft to return, a file
would be opened and given a designation comprising a single letter and six digits.
The files for LM342 were P.407954/43 and for DV202, P.407629/43. All information
regarding the aircraft was included and once the aircraft was confirmed as lost
then the personal files of each crew member were added. These files could be
extensive, covering the entire career of the crewman concerned from the point
at which he attested to the point that he was listed as missing. The files included

Top: The crew of DV202 with their Lancaster B III. From left to right – Les Prendergast, Tommy Weston, Bill Quance, Len McDermott, Stan Shaw, Reg Harding and Peter Pynisky. *(Towlson Family Collection)*

Above: The crew of DV202 at RAF Dunholme Lodge. Back row from left – Stan Shaw, Len McDermott, Les Prendergast and unknown airman. Front row from right – Bill Quance, Peter Pynisky, Reg Harding, Tommy Weston and unknown airman. *(Towlson Family Collection)*

No. 44 Squadron airmen with a Lancaster at RAF Dunholme Lodge, Summer 1943.
(Towlson Family Collection)

Reg Harding, the nineteen-year-old Canadian pilot of DV202. *(Harding Family Collection)*

Opposite page, clockwise from top: Les Prendergast on leave, with his brother;
on leave in Liverpool at the home of his parents Harold and Margaret and brother Andrew;
Les out for a stroll with Reg Harding, Summer 1943. *(Authors Collection)*

Peter Pynisky, Bill Quance and Stan Shaw relaxing by the well at RAF Dunholme Lodge.
(Towlson Family Collection)

Below: An excerpt from a memorial booklet produced by the Sydney Academy, Nova Scotia where Peter Pynisky had been a student. Produced in 1947, the reported date of his loss is incorrect.
(Authors Collection)

W/O PETER PYNISKY

Peter came to the Academy from Holy Redeemer School in the Fall of 1937, and he immediately made his presence felt around the building and particularly on the football field. He was a member of the championship team of 1938-39. After completing Grade Eleven, he left school and was employed at the Steel Plant. From there he enlisted in the R.C.A.F. in 1941. He trained in Canada, and went overseas in April 1942. He was reported missing on his twenty-third Operational Flight over Germany in July, 1943. his parents are Mr. and Mrs. Steven Pynisky of 2 Ferris Street, Sydney, Nova Scotia. His widow is the former Rhoda Foster of New Marston, Oxford, England.

Bill Quance in his flying suit, fur-lined boots and gloves, and wearing his parachute harness.
(Quance Family Collection)

Above: A rare photograph of Stan Shaw from his youth. He can be seen on the left in a church play, aged ten. Right: Stan Shaw with his wife Elsie on their wedding day, 5 June 1933. (*Towlson Family Collection*)

Publicity photograph taken of John Nettleton's crew. Stan Shaw and Bill Quance flew with the crew while Reg Harding was recuperating from an injury. Stan Shaw can be seen second from the right and Bill Quance third from the right. (*Towlson Family Collection*)

Tommy Weston with his new bride, Florence, in a photographic studio in 1935.
(Goldstone Family Collection)

Tommy clearly enjoying his honeymoon with his happy bride Florence in Blackpool, 1935.
(Goldstone Family Collection)

Top: Tommy with his daughter, Barbara, having a picnic in 1938. Main picture: With Barbara on a visit to the Houses of Parliament in 1939. Above: Enjoying his leave in 1941 with Barbara in the garden of their house in Northenden, South Manchester. *(Goldstone Family Collection)*

Above: The crew of LM342 being interviewed at RAF Bottesford by a reporter from the *Daily Sketch* on their return from a raid to Dortmund on 24 May 1943. This date was chosen as it was Australia Day and No. 467 Squadron was nominally an RAAF squadron. They are from the left – Francis Garrett, Daily Sketch reporter, Adam Brand, Frank Grey, Vivian Smith, Ron Carter, Derrick Fielden and their pilot, Squadron Leader Alfred Sydney 'Ray' Raphael. Note that the left-hand side of the background has been censored. Below: The crew received copies of the photograph from the *Daily Sketch*, which they all signed behind their position on the photograph. *(Shern Family Collection)*

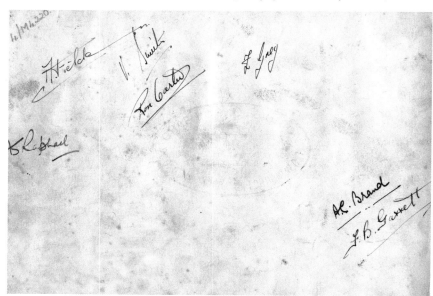

Left: Derrick Fielden aged three is seen on the left with his big sister Joan in this studio image taken around 1923. Joan Fielden is the mother of Jackie McLeod, the author's wife. *(Authors Collection)*

Above: Derrick aged around fifteen relaxing on the beach near his grandparents' house on Hayling Island. Right: Derrick with his younger brother Colin and big sister Joan pictured shortly before the outbreak of war. *(Authors Collection)*

Derrick Fielden in his 'civvies' taken in 1939 not long before his RAF uniform became his usual attire.
(Author's Collection)

Derrick, dressed to impress, out for a walk with his French girlfriend in June 1939.
(Author's Collection)

Above: Derrick taking a break from the war back at his parents' house in Chandlers Ford. Right: Derrick with his siblings, Joan and Colin. Also on the picture is fellow airman and friend, Ron.
(Author's Collection)

Above: Derrick, pictured here in Spring 1943 with his sister's nursing friend, Pat. His previously well starched uniform is looking a little war weary by now. *(Author's Collection)*

Right: Francis Garrett in the early part of his gunnery training RAF Stormy Down, Bridgend in 1941. Seen here in his rugby kit. Far right: Francis Garrett on leave in 1943 visiting Home Farm in Clifton, Oxfordshire which had been the family's home for generations.
(Garrett Family Collection)

Frank Grey aged 14 in 1937 wearing his school uniform in Newbridge, South Wales. This was less than six years before he was killed at Peenemünde, six weeks after his twentieth birthday. Inset: Frank Grey had volunteered at the age of 18 and was sent to No. 5 Initial Training Wing in Torquay, Devon.

(Shern Family Collection)

Vivian Smith with wife Megan enjoying some time together at the beach. Inset: Vivian Smith and Megan. He was killed about a month before they were due to celebrate their first wedding anniversary. (*Wendy De Lisle Collection*)

Below, left: Ron with his father, Captain George Carter, pictured not long after joining the Empire Air Training Scheme. His father serving in the RCMP volunteered to rejoin the army taking care of German POWs in Canadian camps. Below, right: The last photograph of Ron Carter in Canada before embarking in a convoy to Scotland. Here seen in his rather smart 'civvies'. Bottom: A studio photo of Ron Carter which he signed and sent back to his family in Canada. *(Barrie Carter Collection)*

Right: Ray Raphael, left, with No. 467 Squadron commander Cosme Gomm who would be killed on 15/16 August 1943 resulting in Raphael being appointed as acting AOC – a position he held for a scant two days. *(Vincent Holyoak Collection)*

Above: Ray Raphael on the right enjoying a few beers at RAF Bottesford in June 1943. *(Vincent Holyoak Collection)*

Left: Martyn Hope Parry (right), No. 467 Squadron Bombing Leader, who fatefully decided to go with the crew of LM342 on its last operation. He was buried on the airfield at Peenemünde. *(Vincent Holyoak Collection)*

1353125 SERGEANT
A. C. BRAND
AIR GUNNER
ROYAL AIR FORCE
18TH AUGUST 1943 AGE 34

SACRED
OF

Adam Brand was the first to bail out of LM342, landing in the sea. His body was washed 20 miles down the coast and was buried by the Germans at Swinemunde. In 1948 his body was exhumed and reinterred in the Poznan Old Garrison Cemetery in Poland. He is the only airman from LM342 and DV202 to have a recognised grave. *(The Wargraves Photographic Project)*

Steven Cassell, wireless operator aboard Lancaster ED647 which crashed in the sea off Peenemünde. His body washed ashore on 30 August near the airfield and was buried where it was found. One other crewman washed up in Poland and no trace of the other five was found. *(Author's Collection)*

Thomas Brocklehurst (on the far right) was an air gunner on Lancaster ED805 which crashed in the sea on the approach to the target. His body washed ashore by the airfield and was buried where he was found. *(Author's Collection)*

The wreckage of the Lancaster in the Kölpien-See at Peenemünde. Though this is widely viewed as being the wreckage of DV202 there is no definitive proof. The Air Historical Branch of the RAF has stated that it is likely to be the wreckage of LM342. The wreckage consists of a section of the fuselage and the port wing complete with the port inner engine, which is submerged in silt. A definitive identification could be made by examining the engine. This would be a costly and complicated exercise requiring specialist divers and equipment. *(Mike McLeod)*

A view from the roof of The Peenemünde Historical Technical Museum looking north towards Kölpien-See. Recreations of a V1 and V2 can be seen in the foreground. *(Mike McLeod)*

Looking north over the south shore of the Kölpien-See where the bodies of Francis Garrett, Alfred Sydney Raphael, William Quance, Stan Shaw and Leslie Prendergast are buried. *(Mike McLeod)*

Another view over the south Shore of the Kölpien-See. A solitary wooden cross and poppy commemorate the area of the grave site. *(Mike McLeod)*

A view of the airfield where Frank Grey, Martin Parry, Derrick Fielden and two unknown airmen are buried. The image shows hardened aircraft shelters built by the Russians during the Cold War.
(Mike McLeod)

The graves of three of the airmen who were killed on the Peenemünde raid who had been buried by the Germans in Greifswald Cemetery. They are among the 84 bodies recovered by the MRES in 1948 from the area surrounding Peenemünde and reburied in the Imperial War Graves Commission Cemetery in Berlin. *(Mike McLeod)*

dental records, medical history, personal assessments, details of next of kin, occupation and address of parents etc. They included a full list of personal items, and even outstanding mess bills. Everything was covered; nothing was left out. Sometimes they could contain some 400 pages or more.

It was important that information regarding the fates of the crews was contained in the files so that they could be referred to in future, should the remains of the aircraft (or the bodies of the men) be found. If the men still remained 'missing', then it was also important that any/all information pertaining to their loss was kept and could be referred to after the war when the search for all missing aircrew with no known graves would begin.

Information regarding lost aircraft came from many sources, both official and unofficial, and from friend and foe alike. They included reports on the ground from local resistance units, interrogation reports from returning aircrew who had escaped or evaded capture after bailing out, and RAF reconnaissance photographs taken and developed within hours of the operation being completed.

The greatest and most productive source of information came from the Germans themselves, though it was not always given from the kindness of their hearts. Lists of airmen who had been captured or confirmed as dead could be broadcast on German radio for propaganda purposes, in the full knowledge that the British were listening. The information was noted by the Air Ministry, but also closely followed by the relatives of the airmen who were missing.

A more formal source of information, although still dependent on the Germans, was the information they provided through the International Red Cross and known as the 'Totenliste' (literally 'death roll').

Throughout Germany, all incidents involving Allied aircraft that were shot down or crashed were reported to the area Luftgaukommando (Luftwaffe Command). These reports would be collated and a file opened for each incident. Telegrams would be sent to London giving the basic details of each casualty.

Periodically a Totenliste would be compiled containing the details of up to 200 casualties. Depending on the information available, against each entry would be given a name, rank, number, date of death and burial details. The location of the death was not given for security reasons. In the first four years of the war, the bodies of Allied aircrew were treated with the same respect that would be afforded to dead Luftwaffe aircrew shot down over England. Burials were generally carried out in local cemeteries in a military service, complete with wreaths and a rifle salute. (Later in the war, with the volume of dead RAF and USAF aircrew mounting, and time, resources and sympathy ebbing away, burials became rather more haphazard affairs, making the subsequent recovery of the men by the Missing Research and Enquiry Units (MREU) that much harder.)

In 1939, the German government established the Wehrmachtauskunfstelle in Berlin, which was to be the conduit to provide information primarily regarding prisoners of war, but also casualties in accordance with the Geneva Convention. In 1943, the section dealing with Allied casualties was relocated to Meiningen in the south-western state of Thuringia. It was from here that the Totenliste was forwarded to the offices of the International Commission of the Red Cross (ICRC) in Geneva. The ICRC, being a neutral organisation in a neutral country, passed casualty lists and names of POWs in both directions. Upon receipt of the Totenliste in Geneva, they would in turn be forwarded to the British Red Cross in Belgrave Square.

Having received the initial telegrams and subsequent Totenliste from Geneva, the British Red Cross would then inform the Casualty Section of the Air Ministry where they would be translated and grouped into crews. This information would then be added to the file relating to each lost aircraft. From there, information would then be passed back to the Red Cross together with details of the next of kin of each dead airman and their fellow crew members. They would then write to all of the crew members' families. One such letter, dated 10 November 1943, was received by the family of Derrick Fielden, wireless operator in the crew of Ray Raphael, a full three months after he had gone missing:

Dear Mr Fielden

We very much regret that up to the present we have not received any information about your son, Flight Sergeant D Fielden 751496, but we think we should tell you that an official German report has reached us through the International Red Cross Committee at Geneva concerning the crew in which he was a member.

From this report, received in a telegram from the organization in Geneva, it would appear that on the 18 August, 1943, six airmen lost their lives in a disaster that involved two of our aircraft. Of your son's crew, the names and service numbers of Acting Squadron Leader Raphael and Flight Sergeant Garrett are given and also those of four of the crew of the second aircraft. No mention is made of your son.

Further enquiries are being made on your behalf, and you will be notified at once if any reply is received.

We are deeply sorry to send this news and realise how much it will add to your anxiety, but we should not feel justified in withholding it from you, nor do we think you would wish us to do so.

It was signed by the chairman, Margaret Ampthill.[38]

The letter was of little or no comfort for the family of Derrick Fielden, and use of the phrase '… *a disaster that involved two of our aircraft …*' led the family to believe, quite wrongly, that the aircraft had been in a collision. It had not. Two aircraft had come down in close proximity to one another, and the casualties reported in a single document. It was a misunderstanding that was to have unfortunate consequences in the subsequent search for the missing men.

The parents of Ray Raphael and Francis Garrett received a similar letter from Lady Ampthill. Percy Raphael wrote to Derrick's sister: '*This morning I received the attached letter from Lady Ampthill wherein you will see that up to 20 November there was no news of any other members of my son's crew, so there is still great hope for your brother. Please accept for yourself and convey to your mother and father my very best wishes and assure them that as soon as I receive any further information I will pass it on to you.*'

Percy Raphael took it upon himself to correspond with all of the members of his son's crew where possible. On 23 November, he wrote to the father of Ron Carter, Ray Raphael's Canadian navigator:

I received your very charming letter of 30 October, and your son Ronald seemed to be of the same calibre as my boy – God rest his soul.

What actually happened I don't know, but I have received a letter from the Red Cross telling me that my son had lost his life.

Up to this morning, 23 November, 10-30, there was still no news of your boy or any other members of the crew except F/Sgt Garrett. I am in constant touch with the Air Ministry and the Red Cross, and they all have instructions to notify me the moment they have news of any of the crew. As soon as I receive any information, no matter what it may be, I will cable you, but in the meantime there is nothing further I can do.

Naturally my wife and I are heartbroken. Alfred was our only child – a lovely young fellow – clean and everything a man should be. We are trying hard to pull ourselves together and face the world with what interest still remains for us. I sincerely hope that you will get better news than we have had and I look forward to being the bearer of the same.

While Ray Raphael's father had the benefit of being in London, and therefore 'closer' to the administrative machinations that would reveal the fate of his son, it was more frustrating for the parents of the missing men who lived overseas. Communication was not always as 'joined up' as it could have been through official channels, and relatives often pieced together snippets of information from other families in order to frame a complete picture of what had happened to their sons. Unfortunately, this often led to further misunderstandings and frustrations, as evidenced by a letter sent by Reg Harding's father to the Department of National Defence for Air in Ottawa dated 12 December 1943:

Re Pilot Officer Reg C Harding J17338. Now Missing.

We have received air graph messages from three members of English families concerning their boys, forming the crew of this missing plane. We also have some word from above source re one Canadian crew member Peter Pynisky of Nova Scotia. These people tell us a collision occurred between two planes over Germany during an attack on Peenemünde on the night of 17/18 August. The plane piloted by my son had four killed: Pynisky – Canadian, Prendergast, Shaw and Quance of the RAF.

The other plane had two killed, this information seems to be quite definite. This word was received by their families about 18 November.

It makes us wonder if official circles have any clue as to what happened to the three other crew members. It is remarkable that these three men – Bomb Aimer, Flight Engineer, and Pilot, who are not reported, formed the front end of this plane's crew. Did this plane land or did it explode in mid air?

Any information you may have on this will be very welcome to us.

Squadron Leader Wilfred Gunn,[39] the RCAF Casualties Officer for the Chief of the Air Staff in Ottawa replied to Mr Harding Sr by return, and then again on 20 January 1944:

Further to my letter of 22 December, a reply has now been received to the enquiry made overseas regarding your son and other members of the crew. The message states that the only information available was received from the International Red Cross Society at Geneva and stated that on 18 August 1943, six personnel were reported to have lost their lives, their names being Squadron Leader Raphael, Pilot Officer Prendergast, Flight Sergeant Shaw, Flight Sergeant Pynisky, Flight Sergeant Garrett, and Sergeant Quance. As these airmen were members of the crews of two aircraft, it was assumed both aeroplanes crash[ed] together.

Official German information recently received advises that Flight Sergeant Pynisky was buried on 21 August at Kolpinsee in the province of Mecklenberg [sic], North Germany.

Again, the ambiguous phrase referencing the assumption that both aircraft crashed together served only to confuse subsequent enquiries. Mr Harding's understandable desperation for news spilled over in a later letter, in April 1944, by which time his son had been presumed killed in action:

Will you please answer the following questions for us regarding our son who is missing. Was the Lancaster my son was piloting at the time of the crash found on shore, or did it crash in the sea, or were the members of the crew found on land or floating on the water?

Have any other crew members of the two planes apparently involved ever been heard from? If so are they in prison or free? Is it the opinion of the RCAF these men are alive in enemy country or if they may be, in the sea?

If you can give us any facts, we will be grateful to you and all others who are working on this matter.

Mr Harding clearly had no real understanding of the situation in Europe at the time, or the vast numbers of missing aircrew enquiries being handled. A reply was received in the first week of May:

I am indeed sorry that no additional information has been received regarding your son since my letter of 20 January 1944.

The International Red Cross Society at Geneva will communicate all particulars that are given to them by the enemy. Such information is persistently followed up by the International Red Cross in an endeavour (sic) to secure every detail. Unfortunately, as it is not possible to compel the enemy government to furnish detailed information I feel assured that you will appreciate the difficulties attendant upon any investigation that is made by the IRC, and that it is not known where the aircraft collided. As no information is on record at these headquarters regarding personnel who are not members of the RCAF, I have made enquiries overseas to obtain particulars of the other crew members.

Due to conditions existing in the air warfare being waged over Germany and the lack of any further information, you will understand that it is not possible to form any opinion as to the fate of these members of the crew who are as yet unaccounted for.

Although the Air Ministry now proposes to presume your son's death, I wish to point out that such action is taken for official purposes only and will not affect or diminish in any way the efforts which are being made to secure some trace of your son.

The suggestion that two aircraft had collided had now become a definite state-ment, given apparent official endorsement, even though the Canadian author-ities had no firm evidence to substantiate the claim. It was unfortunate. But it was not the only information to be incorrectly recorded that would cause later difficulties. It seemed even the German authorities could also make mistakes.

An important source and method of recording details of both missing aircraft and men was an official 'Loss Card' collated by the Air Ministry Casualty Section. The process would begin once a loss telegram had been received from the relevant squadron. In the case of LM342, for example, the Loss Card provides the date of the operation, the aircraft type (A Lancaster Mark III), serial number (LM342), squadron (No. 467), base (Bottesford), target (Peenemünde) and route to target. It lists the crew by order of pilot, navigator, wireless operator, flight engineer, bomb-aimer, and the two air gunners. A final space in the column is left for any additional crew members, most often a second pilot, but in this case it is filled by the squadron bombing leader (A3).

On receipt of the Totenliste from the ICRC in Geneva, the names would be sorted into crews and the details of each crew member listed would be added to the Loss Card. In the example of LM342, the names (reading down the Loss Card) were reported on Totenliste 175 and are recorded as follows:

Raphael – Dead 175/112
Grey – Dead 175/108
Garrett – Dead 175/100
Parry – Dead 175/109.

Of the other members of the crew – Ron Carter, Derrick Fielden, Vivian Smith and Adam Brand – the column is left blank. On the rear of the Loss Card, a further narrative is included:

175/100 Garrett 1154625; shot down 18.8.43. b (buried) 24.8.43.
Kölpien-See Südufer (south shore).

175/108-9 Grey 1317456 and Parry 126019 shot down 18.8.43 b. 25.8.43
Peenemünde

175/112 Raphael 68155; shot down 18.8.43. b. 24.8.43 Kölpien-See.

The Air Ministry would helpfully provide map references, where it was possible to do so, to assist with the recovery of bodies at a later date. Unfortunately, there are four lakes with similar names in Germany ('See' translates as 'lake'), and the map reference provided by the British authorities is for the Kolpin-See (as opposed to the Kölpien-See), which is near the town of Waren, in the then province of Mecklenburg, some 100km or so south-west of Peenemünde.

The Loss Card for DV202 similarly listed four of its crew as 'dead', allocating them the following numbers and burial locations in the later narrative (A2):

175/101-103 Shaw S 1576142; Quance W 1213933; Prendergast 1127532
shot down 18.8.43. b 24.8.43 Kölpien-See Südufer (south shore).

175/104 Pynisky P R104462 as above b 21.8.43 Kölpien-See Westufer
(west shore).

The information was transcribed on to the Loss Cards from translations made of the official death lists, and it seems that it is here that the Kölpien-See – which is a comparatively small body of water in Peenemünde – has been confused and wrongly identified as the Kolpin-See in Mecklenburg. The error was to have huge ramifications in the years to come (A4).

As the war progressed, the German's fastidiousness for keeping records was somewhat overtaken by the realities of fighting a losing battle on many fronts – on the ground, at sea and in the air. The overwhelming superiority of the RAF at night, and the USAAF during the day, prompted a change in policy among the German military, the first significant shift coming in 1944 when the Wehrmacht discontinued the custom of providing wreaths for the burials of Allied airmen. A more sinister development was a decree from the Führer, Adolf Hitler, that cast all Allied bomber crews as 'Terror Flieger' (literally 'terror flyers'), a theme enthusiastically adopted by his Minister of Propaganda, Joseph Goebbels. The exact nature of the order has found different interpretations over time, but effectively gave civilians carte blanche to kill any Allied aircrew that fell into their hands. In the event, such incidents were mercifully rare.

Another 'casualty' in the change of policy towards Allied aircrew was the end of the Totenliste system, which became more sporadic by the middle of 1944 and disappeared in its entirety before the year was out. The lack of casualty information reaching the Air Ministry from the Red Cross caused considerable alarm, especially since thinking was already well advanced to use the Totenlisten as primary source material for recovering the bodies of downed aircrew and concentrating them within new military cemeteries (that would become the Commonwealth War Graves).

As the Allies advanced across Europe, documents were captured that added further detail to what was already known. When the American forces entered Meiningen, a town in the southernmost part of the state of Thuringia, they uncovered a treasure trove of paperwork relating to the identification, fate and burial of missing airmen. Crucially, they also identified the sources from which the recorded material was compiled.

Among these documents was a letter sent by the Comité International de la Croix-Rouge to the Oberkommando der Wehrmacht regarding the fate of the two principal crews integral to our story (A7). The letter is dated 3 July 1944 and refers to the names already recorded on Totenliste 175 and whether any subsequent information is available regarding their place of burial, beyond the brief outline already reported. It also asks for any information regarding the other members of their respective crews, and for the first time refers to the burial of three 'unknown' bodies and whether these could be connected to the crews referred to in the letter. The letter, which is marked with the file number EV3924/43, also repeats the error regarding the location of the Kölpien-See. (It should be noted that at this time, Peenemünde was in the state of Pomerania (or Vorpommern) and Mecklenburg was a separate state to the south west. After several name changes under the Russian period of control, the two states were joined to become Mecklenburg-Vorpommern after the collapse of the Soviet Union in 1991.)

The draft response to the letter from the ICRC, and bearing the same file number EV3924/43, was also discovered by American troops, stating that while they had no further information regarding the missing men, they would seek to make further enquiries regarding the three 'unknowns'. Later, in the same handwritten draft, the burial sites of the three 'unknowns' are given as being at the 'dock' (or possibly a mooring) in Peenemünde, on the west edge of the airfield, and on the shoreline by the airfield (A8).[40]

The mention of the airfield is important, and a further telegram captured by the Allies in 1945 begins to show why (A5). The telegram is from the office of the commandant of the airfield at Peenemünde. It is dated to the evening of 24 August 1943 and copied to Dulag Luft Oberusal near Frankfurt (the initial interrogation camp for captured Allied airmen prior to being sent to a main Oflag or Stalag). The main recipient, however, is the Luftgaukommando XI at Blankensee, near Hamburg.

The first part of the telegram relates to the capture of a Sergeant Roy Taylor, who'd bailed out of his No. 15 Squadron Stirling and been taken into custody. Other members of his crew had also been taken prisoner although two others were killed when their aircraft eventually crashed into the sea near Greifswald. They were buried in the local cemetery.

The second half of the telegram refers to the recovery and burial of six bodies from the wreckage of a Halifax (sic) bomber bearing the code 'MK' which had been shot down by a night fighter. A Halifax was easy to confuse with a Lancaster, especially if the aircraft had been all but destroyed, and while no aircraft on the raid carried the squadron code MK, the No. 44 Squadron code was KM. Four of the bodies listed came from the crew of DV202 and listed as Bredergast (Prendergast), Schaw (Shaw), Pyniskyn (Pynisky) and Quance. The fifth is named as Garrett, the rear gunner in LM342. The sixth body could not be identified.

Although rather gruesome, the telegram goes on to note that the bodies were discovered in an advanced state of decay and were buried in the locations they were found. This is unusual, since the normal procedure would have been to take the bodies to a local cemetery. Indeed, some eighty-four airmen who perished in areas adjacent to the target site were buried in local graveyards. The telegram also states that the ID discs of the deceased airmen had been delivered to the commandant at Greifswald airfield prior to being forwarded to Hamburg.

What is potentially of huge significance is that the commander at Peenemünde airfield would only have reported on matters within the secure confines of his establishment, and this provides a vital clue as to where the missing graves could be located. While a translation was made of the telegram a full two years after it was discovered, the source of the information was not provided. It was an omission that again could have given the MREU vital information to narrow their search, for the telegram is at odds with the suggestion that the bodies were buried in Mecklenburg (A6).

One of the most revealing of all sources of post-war information was to be found on captured 'KE' Cards used to document the fate of all Allied airmen, whether dead or held as prisoners of war. Basic information regarding name, rank and number was added to as further facts became available, such as the aircraft they flew and what had happened to it. There were even spaces for their mother's and father's Christian names, such that a full record of each individual could be created.

Among the captured cards is one allocated to Stan Shaw (A9), rear gunner in DV202, and featuring a black stamp to indicate that he was dead. It also features the word 'Tod', underlined, just in case there was any doubt. It is on the KE Card that Shaw's burial date and location are recorded, and on the reverse of the card some additional detail is given that is already known, including a cross-reference to the ICRC letter of July 1944 requesting further information regarding his actual grave. A case number, EV3924/43, has also been added.

Certain facts on Stan Shaw's card have been updated in red, based on additional information provided by the ICRC and reflecting the comparatively honest and open two-way sharing of data that existed at this time. On Ray Raphael's card (also given the case number EV3924/43), similar information has been noted and updated, and his place of burial stated as the Kölpien-See (A11). The burial date given on Frank Grey's KE Card (A10) is stated as being 25 August, a full week after he was shot down and concurring with the report from the

German airfield commander. The location of his grave is given as the Flugplatz (airfield) at Peenemünde.

All of the cards relating to our two principal crews feature the same reference numbers and their graves are listed as being either on the shoreline of the Kölpien-See or in and around the airfield. They complete a substantial audit trail, but one sadly punctuated by critical errors that would lead the men sent to recover their bodies on the wildest of wild goose chases.

Chapter Five

The Searchers

A jeep pulls up outside the Hotel du Parc in Chantilly, 60km to the north of Paris and a young flying officer jumps out, peeling the aviator's sunglasses from his head as he treads wearily to the door. The baking heat of the day, and his grim task as an officer within the Missing Research and Enquiry Service (MRES), has sapped all of his strength, and he is looking forward to a long soak and a longer drink in the mess with Mike, his CO, and his fellow officers. It is, in some ways, a ragtag bunch that includes a pongo Army officer and a couple of Australians, and their mix of military uniforms and colours often cause heads to turn.

Arthur Perks had trained as a navigator in the vast open spaces of South Africa, but had qualified too late to see action. He is still proud, however, of his observer's brevet. On his return home and somewhat out of the blue he had been ordered to report to the Air Ministry at Kingsway and told about a new organisation being formed to look for and recover Allied airmen who had been shot down during the war. It was a difficult and demanding job, he was told, but in the best traditions of the RAF in looking after its own. The Americans, he learned, were doing much the same thing with units of their American Graves Registration Service, and no doubt their paths would cross.[41]

The task was indeed grim. Each of the various Missing Research and Enquiry Units that formed part of the MRES were given designated areas in which to conduct their searches. At the beginning, Arthur had been based in Le Mans, and only recently moved to the attractive town of Chantilly with its famous racecourse. The Hotel du Parc was basic, but comfortable enough, and certainly preferable to sleeping under canvas, however pretty the stars.

The process was now well established. They would be sent Casualty Enquiry letters from the Air Ministry, each one pertaining to the loss of an aircraft and its crew. The letters were based on the casualty files compiled from the initial squadron loss reports, German Totenlisten, captured German documents and – perhaps most helpful of all – the first-hand debriefing/intelligence reports from surviving airmen upon repatriation.

Today, Arthur has been out looking for the burial place of a 26-year-old pilot officer shot down on 9 June 1940. He'd been part of a three-man crew of a Blenheim IV of No. 107 Squadron attacking German armour in the Forêt de Boray. His skipper and wop/AG had made it out in one piece to become prisoners of war but the observer was not so lucky. As it goes, it is one of the easier searches, and after a few discreet enquiries he is directed to a spot in an overgrown grave-yard by a church in Damery, in the beautiful Champagne region of France. The grave of the missing pilot is clearly marked with a simple white cross.

The body of Colin Campbell will still need to be exhumed and full investi-gation report completed to confirm his identity. Then it will be carefully and respectfully moved, to one of the larger commonwealth war graves (under the auspices of what was then known as the Imperial War Graves Commission (IWGC)) being created across France and Germany. In Campbell's case, his exhumed body will rest in a large cemetery in Rouen, alongside those of airmen and soldiers killed in an earlier war.

Arthur and his kind have very little training, considering the work that they do, and do not have the advantages of modern-day forensics. Some limited infrared technology is available but mostly they use instinct and common sense, and whatever they have learned from the police. Sometimes an identity can only be confirmed by a scrap of uniform on a badly burned body and a handful of digits from a known service number printed on the inside of a shirt collar. If they are very lucky, an ID disc may still be found, not unusually in a back pocket or lying loose, or perhaps an Air Ministry watch. Parts of the body can sometimes be missing, and all has to be recorded.

Today the local French villagers have been helpful, but it is not always the case, and he's heard that his colleagues in Germany are having a tougher time. It is understandable that the Germans are not quite so willing to assist finding the men who had destroyed their homes and killed their loved ones. Some, also, have secrets to hide, and a need for the bodies to remain undiscovered.

Arthur has had enough to think about for one day, and heads for the bathroom at the end of the corridor. Tomorrow he will do it all again.

The RAF has a proud reputation for finding and returning its missing men, a reputation that was cemented in the Second World War by the remarkable work of the various Missing Research and Enquiry Units operating across Europe. While Arthur Perks and his colleagues, led by Wing Commander Mike Shaw, searched the villages and towns to the east of Paris and beyond, No. 4 MREU was given the task of locating and recovering bodies in Germany itself. This would have been difficult enough had Germany remained united under the umbrella of a single controlling power. As it was, the Americans, British, French and Russians shared in the country's future, and searches in the Russian Zone were to become especially problematic.

As early as October 1946, No. 4 MREU received a Casualty Enquiry (G872) relating to LM342, shot down in the Russian Zone. The letter listed the aircraft mark and code, and where and on what date it was reported missing. The crew was listed in full, with ranks and service numbers, as well as relative roles. Martyn Parry was listed as the second air bomber. The letter detailed what was known regarding the fate of the men and their possible graves. The Kölpien-See was mistakenly estimated to be in Mecklenburg.

A similar letter (G536) was sent regarding Lancaster DV202, the remains of which were also now thought to be in the Russian Zone. The letters were almost identical, including a map reference for the Kolpin-See (sic). They differed, however, in one very important aspect. The opening paragraph of the second letter included details of all four of the Lancaster's Rolls-Royce Merlin 28 engines. A four-digit manufacturer's serial number was given, alongside a six-digit number from the Air Ministry: Port Outer (PO) 3539/267493; Port Inner (PI) 6505/325794; Starboard Inner (SI) 6098/325522; and Starboard Outer (SO) 6090/325519. These numbers would become significant later.

At much the same time that the letters were being received by the OC No. 4 MREU, a dedicated detachment (No. 21 Section MRES) was being set up in Berlin specifically to recover bodies that were now in land under Soviet jurisdiction. The man put in charge of this Berlin Detachment was no stranger to the concept of being 'missing in action', for he had himself been posted as 'missing', having been shot down in the Mediterranean in 1942 and finishing up as a prisoner of the Italians. Flying Officer John Willis-Richards had been the only survivor.

Now as Squadron Leader Willis-Richards, he set about his task with great gusto, taking out small advertisements in local German newspapers and receiving crucial information from more than 300 German informants, either in writing or in person. The information was of sufficient quality, in several cases, to quickly resolve a number of enquiries, allowing Willis-Richards and his team to concentrate on the more challenging cases.[42]

The scale of the task, however, should not be underestimated. In one of his first reports to the Chief of Air Division, RAF, dated 9 November 1946, Willis-Richards listed the towns in and around Berlin in the Russian Zone that he and his men had visited, travelling a distance of some 2,000 miles in pursuit of their objectives.

Their search areas were divided into administrative districts called 'Kreise', the German equivalent to the French 'Departements'. It was not until October 1947, though, that the RAF men were given permission to search Kreis Grimmen, one of the first areas associated with aircraft lost on the Peenemünde raid. Flight Lieutenant Herbert and a small team found none of the missing men, but spent valuable hours gaining useful intelligence on possible burial sites. It would be many months before they were allowed to return.

On 22 April 1948, permission was obtained from the Russian authorities to enter the area known as Kreis Waren, in Mecklenburg, to search for the missing men in the Kölpien-See. The administrative error on the Loss Cards and subsequent correspondence several years earlier was at last coming home to roost. On the 28th of the month, Flight Lieutenant Bernard Aptroot and his team spent three days scouring the area. The time spent was not entirely fruitless; the dead men from three other missing aircraft were recovered during the search, but not a single man from LM342 or DV202. Doubtless Aptroot, an astute and intelligent search officer, thought it odd that six members from two different crews would have been found together so far from the target area.

According to the information detailed in the Totenliste, the largest concentration of bodies buried after the Peenemünde raid were to be found in Kreis Greifswald. But it was not until late July that Flight Lieutenant Chancellor Drysdale was allowed in on a three-day sortie that enabled him to recover no fewer than sixty-one bodies from cemeteries in Greifswald and Wieck.

In the middle of August, Drysdale returned to the area and extended his search beyond Greifswald and into the Kreise of Grimmen, Franzberg-Barth and the isle of Rügen. Again, he was successful, exhuming thirty-six bodies from various cemeteries that were transported to Berlin and re-buried in the Heerstrasse Cemetery.

The brilliant work of the Berlin Detachment was constantly frustrated by their Russian hosts, and the mutual distrust that existed at the beginning only grew stronger as their work went on. That Willis-Richards and his team achieved the successes that they did was almost entirely down to their own diplomatic efforts in negotiating with Russian officers on the ground, a point made clear in a report by Group Captain Dunn of the Air Ministry in February 1948 after visiting the detachment: 'Our right to search [the Russian Zone] is flimsy; it rests on no contract but has been weaned from the Russians by local diplomacy. It might be withdrawn for no good reason, at any moment.'

His report went on to say that since October 1947, almost 3,000 bodies had been found and 80 per cent identified. This was thanks not only to the skills of the individual officers, but also, interestingly, their close working relationship with officers from Scotland Yard who had provided great assistance in ways of deducing positive identities. His report praised the spirit of the MREU teams, which it said was down to the personal leadership of the OC MRES, Group Captain Eustace Hawkins:

> Group Captain Hawkins has a particularly happy flair for establishing useful friendships, an invaluable quality in this particular post. The searcher officers themselves are keen and enthusiastic. None of them are exceptionally prepossessing but all have the vital spark and real pride in their rather unattractive task. This is quite definitely attributable to Group Captain Hawkins' personal influence. Russian Conducting Officers make special efforts to go with the RAF as opposed to the Army teams. This is because the young ex-aircrew make efforts to be interesting and converse, whereas their army counterparts, who are mostly elderly ex-rankers, find conversation in any language too strenuous and therefore sit in their transport like bumps on a log until the long day is over![43]

The secrecy around the Peenemünde site, and especially the airfield that was now occupied by the Soviet Air Force, was used by the Russians as a tool to hamper the British recovery efforts. The Berlin Detachment had records of at least eight burials in the area (the Kreis Usedom-Wollin, later to be renamed Kreis Wolgast), in addition to those it knew about in and around the Kölpien-See. Permission to search this area, however, was denied. To add to the confusion, a further body of water, also known locally as the Kolpin-See, was also discovered some 20km south-east of Peenemünde in the Kreis of Usedom-Wollin. It made no odds;

the British were not allowed in. They were also told that Peenemünde airfield had been completely destroyed, and the site of the potential graves was now a huge crater. This could not be true. The reported burial locations were scattered over several square miles. By the end of 1948, No. 4 MREU had long since been disbanded (the cost of keeping so many units in the field could not be met indefinitely), and No. 21 Section MRES found itself as an autonomous unit, still with plenty of work to do, and comprising a team of six officers and seven airmen, helped out by occasional German labour as required.

Willis-Richards and his team continued to be kept under close scrutiny, their work often compromised by last-minute changes to agreed timetables or accompanying liaison officers falling suddenly ill. While the relationship with the Soviet headquarters in Karlshorst was considered both cooperative and helpful, the same was not always the case with the local Kreis commanders. The Berlin Detachment adjusted their operations policy accordingly, covering more than one Kreis per trip. It meant working longer hours but went some way to offsetting the reduced number of trips that the Soviet authorities allowed.

At the start of the New Year, 1949, the detachment helped to produce a schedule of burials showing the state of the investigation into the aircraft and crews lost in the Peenemünde raid. By this point they had recovered the bodies of ninety-six airmen, of whom eleven could not be identified. A further eighty-four were found in local cemeteries adjacent to Peenemünde and twelve in Poland.

All of the bodies recovered had been buried by the German authorities, the only exception being that of Squadron Leader Richard Todd-White of No. 49 Squadron, whose body was washed up on the shores of the Swedish island of Gotland, some 270 miles (430km) north-east of Peenemünde where it was interred by the neutral Swedes. (His identity was in part confirmed by a cigarette case inscribed to him by his wife.)

For the loss of Reg Harding and his crew in DV202, the schedule[44] notes that '... there appear to have been six burials in isolated graves by the Kolpin See (sic) (fourteen miles ESE of Peenemünde). If these graves have not been found, a further search is required. The phrase "buried in the place where they fell" is read to mean that these members bailed out and were killed. The Kolpin See is by the sea and the remaining members are concluded to have been lost at sea.' Prendergast, Quance, Shaw and Pynisky are all confirmed as being buried on the south or west shore of the lake.

For the loss of Ray Raphael and his crew in LM342, Raphael and Garrett are

identified as being presumed buried by the side of the Kolpin-See, and Adam
Brand is known to have been buried in Poznań, Poland, five years after his
battered body came ashore. Smith, Carter and Fielden are presumed to have no
known graves, and were probably lost at sea, whereas the remaining crew members, Grey and Parry, were probably buried by the Peenemünde airfield, which
has since been blown up by the Russians. The site of the graves, the report
suggests, is now a crater, a fact we know not to be true.[45]

Three other aircrew need to be introduced to our story at this time, as their names
feature in the list of those who are recorded as being buried (or likely buried)
in the former Russian military zone.

Reg Harding's aircraft had not been the only Lancaster of No. 44 Squadron
to fail to return to Dunholme Lodge after the raid. Two other Lancasters were
also missing: JA897 H-Howe flown by Pilot Officer John Drew, RAFVR; and
W4935 M-Mother, flown by Pilot Officer Robert Campbell.

Drew's aircraft was shot down by Leutnant Peter Spoden of 6./NJG5. Spoden,
like the rest of the night-fighter force, had been late to arrive but was almost
immediately in the action. He easily picked out a Lancaster and attacked from
astern, aiming at the engines and setting one of the wings on fire. Moments later
it crashed, the whole incident taking less than two minutes from interception
to victory. Killed with their 33-year-old skipper were five of the crew: Sergeant
Joseph Bassett, Sergeant Tim James (from southern Rhodesia), Flight Sergeant
John Jopling, Sergeant James Reid (a nineteen-year-old Scot), and Pilot Officer
Sam Rudkin. There was only one survivor, the rear gunner, William Sparkes.
The crew was reportedly on its seventh operation.[46]

Robert Campbell's aircraft M-Mother was recorded as being within the first
twenty to be shot down, crashing into the sea. Whereas the fates of most of
Campbell's crew have been accounted for, the whereabouts of the mid-upper
gunner – Sergeant Hugh MacAninch – remains something of a mystery. The
mystery stems from a confusion of contemporary reports: the first (Totenliste
175/139) states that his body washed ashore at Peenemünde and he was buried
there on 30 August. (The aircraft had come down in the Baltic between the island
of Rügen and the Peenemünde peninsula.) A second report, however, asserts
that his body was washed ashore on 18 August at Zinnowitz, some eight miles
south-east of the target, and was buried at Peenemünde on 6 September.

(To add even further to the confusion, on the Runnymede memorial his name is commemorated as missing, along with five other members of his crew. Only one member of the crew has a known grave, that of the rear gunner, Sergeant Philip, whose body was washed ashore on the island of Rügen and initially buried at Klein Zicker on 31 August 1943. The body was subsequently exhumed, identified, and reinterred at the Berlin Military Cemetery in 1948.)

On Totenliste 208/44, the name of Sergeant Thomas 'Brock' Brocklehurst, the 29-year-old rear gunner in Squadron Leader Richard Todd-White's Lancaster ED805 (S-Sugar), appears. Operating out of Fiskerton, No. 49 Squadron had a bad night of it, losing four crews with plenty of experience between them. Todd-White, who had only recently joined the squadron, was reportedly flying one of the first operations of his second tour.

Todd-White was buried in Sweden. His body had taken almost four months to finally come to rest. The body of Brock's fellow air gunner, nineteen-year-old Sergeant George Humble, was washed ashore more speedily and buried, later, in Poznań, next to that of Adam Brand. Of the rest of the crew, all were presumed lost at sea. Brock, however, was recorded as being buried in Peenemünde, his body having been found the day after the raid. A subsequent note on the relevant Loss Card says he was buried by the Peenemünde airfield but that the site was subsequently 'blown up' by the Russians. (The author of the note ponders whether this was deliberate or the result of ground fighting in the spring of 1945.[47])

The third of our final airmen is Sergeant Stephen Cassell. Cassell, a married man from St Helens, was the wireless operator in a No. 100 Squadron crew skippered by a New Zealander, Flying Officer Spiers. Their Lancaster, ED647, was brought down on the run-up to the target area, and all on board were believed killed. Totenliste 175/138 advised that Cassell's body had been recovered and buried in Peenemünde on 30 August. A KE Card was also completed to that effect, confirming that he was officially buried by the German authorities. In between being shot down and his remains being found, his wife gave birth to a daughter he would never see. Four years later, the body of the rear gunner, Sergeant John Francis, was one of those exhumed in Gdynia by the Berlin Section of the MRES. He was reinterred in the Malbork Commonwealth War Cemetery. John Francis is the only crew member not to feature on the Runnymede memorial, despite Stephen Cassell's burial also being advised.

From the bodies recovered, the work of the MRES, and the evidence presented through the Totenlisten, RAF Loss Cards, KE Cards and burial schedules, at least fifteen men lay buried in Peenemünde (A12):

From DV202:

Shaw, Quance and Prendergast	buried on the south shore of the Kölpien-See
Pynisky	buried on the west shore of the Kölpien-See

From LM342:

Garrett	buried on the south shore of the Kölpien-See
Raphael	buried on the east shore of the Kölpien-See
Grey, Parry, Fielden	buried by Peenemünde airfield

From ED647:

Cassell	buried on Peenemünde shoreline

From W4935:

MacAninch	buried on Peenemünde shoreline

From ED805:

Brocklehurst	buried on Peenemünde shoreline

Three 'unknown airmen':

TL 175/106	buried on Peenemünde airfield (shore)
TL 175/107	buried on Peenemünde airfield (western edge)
TL 175/110	buried by Peenemünde dock.

While much of this information was known to the authorities at the time, by the spring of 1949, the RAF had to finally concede that it could not extend any further resources to the Berlin Section of the MRES. The actions of the Russians had rendered any future efforts pointless.[48]

It is 22 April 1949. The location is the Victoria Hotel, Northumberland Avenue, London. The once-splendid venue has lost some of its lustre and sparkle since being taken over by the War Office in 1940. Named to commemorate the Golden Jubilee of Queen Victoria, the hotel has entertained the great and the good in British and global society since opening in 1897. Before the war it was a particular favourite of the Americans, drawn to its palatial and luxurious rooms and its close proximity to the city. Ornate dining rooms and a magnificent banqueting suite are key features that have impressed and served well-heeled guests for many years, but now its rooms have been given over to drab khaki and the brutal ordinariness of military service.

In room 104, a team of senior searchers is assembling. Apart from Arthur Beckess, a civilian from the Air Ministry (Casualty section), they are all military men in khaki and blue. Squadron Leader Alfred Sinkinson[49] is a colleague from the Air Ministry, while Major Vincent and Captain Taylor are representing the Army. Vincent is the Deputy Assistant Director of Graves Registration and Enquiries (DAD GR & E), Berlin, while Taylor is representing the Prisoners of War and Graves (PW & G) department of the War Office. The two senior men in the room are Group Captain Eustace Hawkins, commanding the MRES in Berlin, and Lieutenant Colonel Frederick Hallowes, an officer of equal rank and stature, who is also from PW & G.

With the usual pleasantries exchanged, the six men take their seats while the senior Army man outlines the current situation in Germany. The agenda is immediately obvious as Hallowes outlines the proposed plans from the War Office for the rundown and final disbandment of the Army Graves Services in Berlin. All of the cemeteries in Germany, he explains, have now been handed over to the IWGC with the exception of the Heerstrasse Cemetery in Berlin. The RAF are still working on the Reichswald and Rheinberg Cemeteries[50] although that work is nearly completed barring a few minor anomalies and 'adjustments' that still need addressing.

Hallowes also says that there remain a number of isolated graves in Mecklenburg, Saxony, Brandenburg and Saxony-Anhalt whose locations are known, but have not yet been concentrated owing to the long distances involved and the shortage of petrol. There are a number of graves in the Soviet Zone that it has not been possible to find, and in particular the fifteen that are believed to be at the Peenemünde rocket site that the Russians have now demolished.

There are anything up to 200 graves in the province of Thuringia, also in the

Soviet Zone, but the Russians are refusing access, and in East Prussia there are known to be a further seventy-one graves (sixty-nine RAF and two Army) that have yet to be recovered. An approach has been made to the Russian authorities in Berlin to allow for a disinterring team to enter the region, but it appears that the Soviets in Berlin are not sufficiently competent to deal with the request. Poland, on the other hand, has been cleared of all known British and Commonwealth graves, and the bodies concentrated in three war cemeteries (Marlbork, Cracow and Poznań).

Having provided the overview, and invited comment, the lieutenant colonel moves to the main business of the day. He announces that his team (AG3/PW & G) will be disbanded on 30 June 1949 and that only a small section from the branch will remain, under the ultimate control of the Director of Personal Services. This section, to be commanded by Captain Taylor, will be responsible for clearing up any residual questions relating to Army graves and prisoners of war. Any field work is to be completed by the 30th, and the final disbandment of the Army Graves Service, Berlin, will be final by the end of July.

Hallowes feels it is necessary to explain the rationale behind the decision to disband the service, and cites the worsening situation with the Russians, and the unlikelihood of being granted further permission to search for war dead in their land. This does not mean that all hope has been surrendered; an approach has been made to the Soviets to search Thuringia and a similar contact made to insert a disinterring team into East Prussia, albeit that the latter required a convoluted communication involving the War Office, the Foreign Office and the British Ambassador in Moscow.

Regarding the replacement of personnel in Army Graves Units working in the Soviet Zone, Hallowes thinks it is extremely doubtful that the Russians will agree to any such replacement taking place.

At a practical level, there is much to be done, and Hallowes outlines a timetable for withdrawal and a proposed deadline to make further representations to obtain entry into Thuringia.

Further views and comment are invited through the chair. Group Captain Hawkins says that the Russians have indicated that they will consider the entry of a disinterring team into Thuringia if and when the British have completed their work in the recovery of all other graves in the Soviet Zone. Hawkins proposes that every effort should be made to complete this work as soon as possible.

Squadron Leader Sinkinson also speaks. He suggests that the chances of being granted permission to search in East Prussia are most unlikely in the short term, given his previous experience and knowledge of requests that have to be channelled through the Foreign Office. The chair agrees that it is reasonable to delay disbandment to search for the seventy-one graves in East Prussia if permission is granted before the end of July. The group captain states that the MRES in Berlin will be run down by 30 September.

The meeting adjourns, and the military men once again go through the ritual of goodbyes. The hotel has doubtless been the scene of many important meetings and decisions, but for the fifteen families of the fifteen men buried in Peenemünde, it is a critical one. No mention has been made of searching the Kolpin-See, fourteen miles south of Peenemünde, or even the Kölpien-See at Peenemünde itself.

The senior men appear to have accepted that the graves at Peenemünde have been destroyed.

A letter from the Air Ministry to the Imperial War Graves Commission dated 15 September 1949, just two weeks before the final disbandment of the RAF's recovery efforts in Germany, closes the case once and for all on the crew of Lancaster DV202. Paragraph three reads: 'There seems little hope of further permission being granted by the Soviet Authorities to search officers of the Missing Research Organisation [sic] to conduct investigations in Mecklenburg for the purpose of locating the graves of airmen believed to be buried there.'

The bodies were not, as we know, buried in Mecklenburg but that fact is of little consequence. Bodies remaining in any part of the Soviet Zone were now considered unrecoverable, and as such the seven men – Harding, Weston, Prendergast, McDermott, Quance, Shaw and Pynisky – were to have their names commemorated on a proposed memorial to the missing.

A similar note closes the case on the second aircraft, LM342, and its crew. A memorandum dated 14 October 1949 lists the crew – Raphael, Smith, Carter, Grey, Fielden, Garrett, Parry and Brand – of which only Brand is recorded as having a known grave (his body was moved to Poznań in 1948). It states: 'Exhaustive search and enquiry has failed to reveal the burial places of the remaining seven members of the crew and there is no alternative but to register as shown (i.e. as having 'no known graves'.)

As far as the authorities were concerned, there was nothing else to be done.

Chapter Six
_____

The Lady in the Lake

The loss of Lancasters DV202 and LM342 and the missing men of Peenemünde is inextricably linked with another mystery that has puzzled authors, historians and even the RAF itself ever since it was brought to light some forty years ago. It might simply be thought of as the mystery of the Lady in the Lake.

Aerial photographs taken after the attack and in subsequent years reveal a shape in the Kölpien-See, which is unmistakably that of an aircraft. A reconnaissance aircraft captured a photograph of the lake around eleven hours after the Peenemünde raid. In the centre of the photograph the wreckage and detritus of a crashed aircraft can be clearly seen, including both wings. Photographs taken more recently show that it is most certainly a Lancaster. A middle section of the bomber's fuselage is plainly visible, and images taken from above (and in good weather conditions) show the ghostly shadow of a wing submerged under the water.

In 1991, a group of former soldiers and power station workers in and around Peenemünde created an embryonic museum to record the history of site, and the development of the V1 and V2 rockets. Although initially a small operation, it has since grown to become a substantial institution known as the Historisch-Technisches Museum.

Within the museum, a centerpiece is the battered remains of a three-bladed propeller and engine that is consistent with the type of engine used on the Lancaster. Crucially, the engine was reportedly recovered from the west side of the Kölpien-See. In 1992, the curator of the museum contacted the RAF at its base in Gatow to see if the engine could be correctly identified. RAF technicians investigated and reported their findings to the Air Historical Branch (AHB) at

RAF Northolt. The engine is a Packard Merlin XXVIII (V-1650-1) of the kind used by both LM342 and DV202. Although the technicians could not be certain, they reached a conclusion that it was most likely to have been attached to LM342. Information posted on the internet sourced to German researchers, however, claims that the aircraft in the lake is that of DV202. On what basis such a claim was made is difficult to find but was supposedly arrived at on the basis of engine numbers. The AHB, however, is emphatic that this cannot be the case, and the 'Lady in the Lake' is not DV202. Sebastian Cox, Head of the AHB, wrote to the relatives in 2010:

> In 1992, we received an enquiry originating from RAF Gatow in Berlin relating to the wreckage in the lake. This stated that the Merlin engine retrieved from the lake had the serial number 600115. I regret to tell you that we have the original signal from 44 Squadron to the Air Ministry indicating that the aircraft failed to return. This lists all four engines and their serial numbers and this number does not match any of those on the signal and we can thus be quite certain that the wreckage in the water near the museum is that of a different aircraft. Unfortunately, and contrary to instructions extant at the time, 467 Squadron did not include the engine numbers for LM342. We believe it is highly likely that the wreckage is in fact that of LM342 but we cannot be certain.

The AHB's conclusion is centred on the serial number being 600115. But what if that is not the serial number at all, but merely a part number? The engine in the museum studied by the RAF technicians had suffered significant damage, and the identification plate is not present. The engine serial number was supposed to be stamped on a particular part of the engine to assist in rebuilding the engine after an overhaul, but it is similarly not there. It is unlikely that the modern-day RAF technicians from Gatow would have been especially familiar with a Lancaster Merlin, and more than possible that they mistook a part number for the serial number. The sump of the engine, for example, bears the part number 601500, a figure that again has no connection to the serial number. But it is the Parts Catalog (sic) of the manufacturers of the engine in Detroit that perhaps gives us our biggest clue. Even a cursory examination of their numbering system shows how the '60' prefix is frequently used.

Previous authors and books have attempted to stake their claim on the fate of the two aircraft: Bill Chorley in *Bomber Command Losses* (Volume 4, 1943) states that DV202 was lost without trace and LM342 crashed in the Baltic while approaching the target. Martin Middlebrook (in *The Peenemünde Raid*) similarly suggests that LM342 crashed into the Baltic and that DV202 rests in the Kölpien-See. Vincent Holyoak, in *On the Wings of Morning* is at odds with both gentlemen, suggesting that it is LM342 (and not DV202) that crashed in the Kölpien-See.

(In the Nachtjagd war diaries, Dr Theo Boiten states that DV202 was shot down by Leutnant Dieter Musset of 5./NJG1 for his second kill of the night. Musset was involved in no fewer than five separate combats that night and was himself shot down and bailed out, breaking both ankles as a result. He was killed in a flying accident in 1945.)

Perhaps it is possible to advance a further theory on what happened to the two aircraft, a theory based on where the fallen men were buried, and which bodies were found.

LM342, on its run-up to the target, is fatally hit, whether by flak or night fighter doesn't matter. Raphael realises their predicament and orders the crew to bail out. Brand, the mid-upper gunner, is the first to go, while they are still over water. He drops down from his guns, clips his parachute to his harness, and bails out from the rear door, which is only a few feet from his position. Next to go are Parry, Grey and Fielden, the two air bombers and the wireless op, most likely from the front escape hatch and now over land. Although they make it out of the aircraft, they are too low for their parachutes to fully deploy. Last to leave the aircraft, but by now with no chance of survival, are the pilot, Ray Raphael, and the rear gunner, Francis Garrett, who make it out from either end of the doomed bomber. Moments later, the Lancaster smashes to earth and explodes.

Six of the crew have thus been accounted for. Only the fate of the seventh and eighth men, the navigator, Ron Carter, and the flight engineer, Vivian Smith, are not known, although we are aware that the bodies of three unknown airmen are buried on the peninsula.[51] One is on the northern coast, virtually in a straight line north from the Kölpien-See. A second is to the north of the Kölpien-See, by the airfield, in the exact same line of track that the aircraft would have taken and the rest of the crew's bodies were found.

Staying with this theory, let us assume that Lancaster DV202 is on a similar flight path when it is attacked by Dieter Musset. Reg Harding, the spirited young Canadian, similarly realises they are fatally hit, and in a split-second decision decides on a radical course of action, to crash land. He sees ahead of him a small body of water, the Kölpien-See, and attempts to ditch. He doesn't make it, the aircraft is too badly damaged and the controls are not responding as they should. Perhaps he, and other members of the crew, are wounded; perhaps one or two of them are already dead.

As the Lancaster hits the water it breaks apart. Some of the men – the two air gunners, Pynisky and Shaw, the wireless operator, Quance, and the navigator, Prendergast – are thrown clear; certainly their bodies are recovered from the water and buried by the side of the lake. Of the pilot, flight engineer (Weston) and air bomber (McDermott), there is no sign. Being in the front of the aircraft and concentrated in the cockpit area, if the crash has not killed then, then they are trapped, with no hope of survival.

It is, of course, only a theory, but one that is supported by at least some of the facts. The Air Historical Branch originally dismissed the possibility that the Lady in the Lake could be DV202 on the basis of serial numbers that didn't match the known serial numbers of the engines associated with that aircraft. But we now believe that the basis of that assumption is flawed. An audit trail of the burial sites associated with Lancaster LM342 would suggest an aircraft whose crew were attempting to bail out, whereas the graves for the crew of DV202 are all concentrated around the water's edge.

Stuart Hadaway of the Air Historical Branch wrote in 2015: 'The close association of the crash sites of Lancasters LM342 and DV202 did cause some confusion at the time and has contributed to do so since. Although there has been significant speculation, including in TV documentaries, there is simply not enough evidence to conclusively identify the two crashed Lancasters in the lake. We have investigated this question extensively in the past without being able to resolve the issue.'

Since writing that letter, further evidence has come to light. An underwater photograph taken of some of the wreckage in the water shows a part with the number D2977, a number that corresponds exactly to the airframe assembly drawings for a Lancaster (and confirmed by the A.V. Roe museum at Woodford). There is also a stamp that appears to read V FSMW.

During construction, a Lancaster would receive many such stamps – primarily inspectors' stamps and manufacturers' stamps. DV202 was built by Metropolitan Vickers; LM342 by A.V. Roe at Yeadon. Investigations are now ongoing to link this stamp with either of our two aircraft.

Chapter Seven

The Archaeologist

Kai Schaake is a professional marine archaeologist and leads the Rügen branch of the National Association of Marine Archaeology. Having lived in the Rügen area for many years, he often operates from the harbour at Peenemünde. He has dived in the lake several times and is familiar with the wreck of the aircraft that lies beneath its cold waters.

In many respects, Kai is a 'typical' archaeologist; his knowledge of, and proximity to, Peenemünde means he is often approached by enthusiasts, historians and fellow authors and journalists keen to expound their latest theories as to the identity of the Lancaster and how it got there. His response is predictably fact based and he takes nothing for granted, as is to be expected of a scientist. Given his expert status, he is not an easy man to pin down or convince, although he keeps an open mind. At first his response to our new information was noncommittal. Only when further evidence was forthcoming, and in particular the details contained in the Loss Cards and the German KE Cards did he appear to share the same 'Eureka' moment: the possibility – indeed probability – that the bodies of the missing airmen are still buried on the site.

A visit from Kai to the home of Mike McLeod proved to be the start of a long research partnership, which is ongoing. The pair pored over many accrued documents and photographs into the early hours of the morning. Kai has a dry sense of humour and a sharp intellect. He is also, if it is not too much of a cliché, Germanically matter of fact. When asked whether there was any likelihood that the bodies could still be found he answered simply: 'Why not?' It was agreed to start looking for the bodies in the area to the south of the Kölpien-See, and specifically the south shore where there are records for four – and probably five

– burials in a defined area of around twenty acres. The other burials are recorded in an area of approximately three square miles, ranging from the airfield to the seashore.

To begin the search, copies of aerial photographs of the area were sourced from the National Collection of Aerial Photography (NCAP) in Scotland, where-upon Mike came across his first hurdle. The quality and scale of the images varied widely. Undaunted, he obtained images from before the raid (as well as after the attack), comparing the two and searching for anomalies and disturbances that might have indicated where a grave had been dug and a body buried.

A particularly fine set of photographs were available, taken less than twelve hours after the raid, but this was before the burials that we know took place a few days (rather than hours) later. Mike focused his research on photographs taken at intervals from October 1943 to early 1945. In doing so, he similarly focused on ruling out aberrations on the images in order to find common anomalies that appeared on one or more of the photographs.

From the original source photography, Kai started to build a computer model (known more formally as a Geographic Information System) comparing and overlaying the contemporary aerial photographs with present-day satellite images. The results were encouraging, with scars and disturbances on land roughly where we expected remains to be found, and of the correct size, dimensions and shape.

It was then, however, that Mike was confronted with another challenge: access-ing the land to dig. While confident of an approximate area where the bodies may be buried, pinpoint accuracy could not be guaranteed. A shovel would not be sufficient; larger machinery would be needed. The area, however, has a seasonal water table which at times makes the area boggy. More importantly, it ruled out the use of heavy machinery or excavating equipment. And to add a further layer of complication, the area is now classed as a nature reserve.

Notwithstanding these difficulties, Mike set about investigating the owner of the land, a task that seemed easy enough on paper but in reality was somewhat more frustrating. Ultimately it transpired the lake is owned by Dr Renner from Hamburg who has a holiday home on the south-east corner of the lake and does not welcome outsiders. He especially does not appreciate visitors who want to dig up his land and his country's past. Fortunately, while he owns the lake, he does not, in fact, own the lake shore, which had recently come under the control of the Deutsche Bundesstiftung Umwelt (DBU) – one of Europe's largest foundations that promotes innovative, exemplary projects in the field of environmental protection. Kai contacted the DBU who were sympathetic to his request to access their land. Indeed, they proved most helpful and granted Kai permission to investigate the area further, subject to certain reasonable restrictions regarding disturbing the wildlife (the site is famous as a home to beavers, ground-nesting birds and migrating geese).

In the summer of 2018, Mike arranged to meet Kai at Peenemünde, and specifically at a tiny chapel that rests between the Kölpien-See and a military museum (set up to commemorate the site and the night of 17/18 August 1943). Having compared images and notes they proceeded to the south shore, narrowly avoiding the attention of a wild boar as they descended the upper bank. Happily, it was a male; a female would have been especially dangerous.

Kai had presented the evidence to a contact at the Rostock University Archaeology Department, and it had been received enthusiastically. It gave the university a unique opportunity to trial a new technique for investigating an archaeological site, combining a 'traditional' survey with the latest geomagnetic technology.

The geomagnetic survey would give the archaeologists a better understanding of the ground composition in the search area. Four specific 'areas of interest' were defined, but their location meant cutting a large swathe of reed beds, which was undertaken by a local farmer under the supervision of an appointed forester. Once this was completed, then the scientific work could take place.

The magnetic survey effectively revealed sixty-four anomalies, worthy of closer investigation. These anomalies were overlaid once again with an aerial shot taken on 14 April 1945, although the referencing process could only be accurate up to a point. The results were, in many ways, disappointing. Most of the anomalies proved to be glacial boulders, stones or gravel, or metal fragments most likely to have come from exploded bombs. Only one anomaly suggested human interference, a disturbance in the ground below the peat base that hinted at an object visible in the April photograph but no longer there today. It had, quite literally, vanished.

While frustrating for Kai and his team, what was equally vexing was the possibility that they were searching in the wrong place or, to be more accurate, that the area they needed to search had 'moved'. The geography of the place had changed significantly in the last seventy years. The water table was much higher than it had been during the war, and rising sea levels had effectively flooded large parts of both the southern and eastern shorelines, significantly reducing their size and area. It appeared that parts of the lake may also have been drained during post-war construction works. It also seemed that the 'Südufer' described in 1943 was not, perhaps, the same south shore that existed today. While confident that the bodies were probably still there, there would be no easy way of finding them.

For the moment, and because of lack of funds, the search for the missing men has been suspended. Initial excitement has had to be tempered with the realisation that the scale of the task may be beyond private means. Provisional plans are in place to employ a cadaver dog to help in the search, a dog that has helped locate other lost souls from various conflicts over the years, as well as tragedies such as Lockerbie. Such highly trained animals work in sympathy with technology and to a very strict protocol to find bodies that might otherwise never be located. There is hope that a search can be made of the shore by the airfield, where the ground is dry, and extend the search to the upper and lower shores.

The authors have written again to the Ministry of Defence Joint Casualty and Compassionate Centre (JCCC), the department tasked with dealing with RAF remains. They have stated that they can only take action once human remains have been found: 'Regrettably we do not have the resources to actively search for the remains.'

This is completely understandable but nonetheless regrettable, and in sharp contrast to the US Defense POW/MIA Accounting Agency, which appears to stop at nothing to recover its fallen men. It not only has a comprehensive database of all Second World War servicemen whose remains were not recovered or identified after the war, but it also has a specific plan to find them. It actively collaborates with historians in researching, investigating and nominating cases for recovery. The US Marines' motto of 'No man left behind' appears to permeate across all of its armed forces in a way that the rest of us can only marvel at.

Was the raid on Peenemünde worth the sacrifice of the men who lost their lives or who returned emotionally scarred from their experience? How much damage was done? Did it delay the Nazi rocket programme and influence the outcome of the war? Such discussions can be as fruitless and frustrating as analysing the success or otherwise of the Dams Raid, but for the sake of completeness, it is interesting to note what the raid achieved.

Contemporary reports suggested the raid was a complete success, or at least as successful as the planners had dared hope. Losses had been lighter than expected and the C-in-C did not have to order the bomber boys to go back, as he had threatened to do, which means he must have been satisfied with the results.

The post-raid report using photographs taken twelve hours after the attack showed many buildings still burning, with damage to the factories and housing for personnel described as 'extremely severe'. In the northern manufacturing area (aiming point 'E'), twenty-seven buildings of medium size, including the senior officers' mess, were completely destroyed and nine others, including some of the largest and most important, were badly damaged. At aiming point 'B', another large building was partly demolished by two direct hits, and another by blast. Many hits were recorded on the railway and railway stock. In the living and sleeping quarters at aiming point 'F', forty huts were flattened and a further fifty gutted by fire, as well as three large barrack blocks blown apart by high explosives (HE). In the labour camp to the south, at least twenty-three of the forty-five large huts were completely destroyed and others damaged.

John Searby, the Master Bomber, did not doubt the success of the night's operation. He recorded in his log book: 'Master of Ceremonies. Night fighters accounted for many of our aircraft in bright moonlight. A good attack and resulted in the destruction of the experimental establishment.'[52]

Arthur Harris, in his autobiography *Bomber Offensive*, wrote that soon after the attack he learned that a good deal of damage had been done and many scientists and important members of staff killed. It was noticeable, he said, that after the attack '... the enemy became much less definite in the threats he uttered about the secret weapons he was preparing for England: in particular, he failed to mention any specific dates when the V weapons could be expected'.

In Harris's view, and partly in response to a US strategic bombing survey that suggested it was not the RAF but rather three subsequent raids by the Americans that did the real damage, there was never any chance of putting a total stop to the Germans' rocket programme. The best that could be achieved was a partial delay. He very well understood the Nazis' abilities to rise from the ashes: 'A single attack could only cause delay for a month or two,' he wrote. 'But in the war of the V weapons, time was everything, and every delay we could cause the enemy, however brief, was thoroughly worthwhile.'

In the *Strategic Air Offensive against Germany 1939–1945* by Sir Charles Webster and Noble Frankland,[53] the authors argue that the attack on Peenemünde '...

did considerable damage but was hardly so successful as was thought to be the case in London'. The essential part of the plant, they argue, was not destroyed, and research and development could continue after only a very short delay. Certainly, while more than 700 people were killed on the ground, and many buildings completely destroyed, some important testing equipment in the east plant and large parts of the west plant escaped serious damage.

From the German perspective, General Dornberger estimated the delay caused to the development of the rockets to be no greater than four to six weeks but, as Webster and Frankland make clear, this is believed to be a personal view rather than one supported by facts. It has, however, been a benchmark figure adopted by previous commentators. Common sense tells us that the transfer of rocket production to the Harz Mountains, and the shift of rocket testing to a new establishment in Poland, must all have taken precious time and resources. The deaths of two important rocket scientists, too, must have had some impact on the programme's progress.

General Fromm, C-in-C of the Reserve Army responsible for Peenemünde was similarly optimistic. Although the Germans initially reported that the production works at Peenemünde had been 'completely destroyed', this view was later revised, possibly under the influence or direction of Hitler's Reichsminister, Albert Speer. Fromm assessed that work could begin again in four weeks.

Goebbels, the Propaganda Minister, was more pessimistic. If his *Diaries* are to be believed, he maintained that preparation had been set back four or even eight weeks.

Despite the RAF's best efforts, Harris's appraisal was entirely correct; production could only, at best, be disrupted. It could not be stopped. The first operational rocket targeted against Britain was fired on 8 September 1944 from a site in Holland. The last was fired on 27 March 1945, by which time some 2,500 rockets had been sent on their one-way journeys of destruction, 517 landing in London, killing around 2,700 civilians. In one attack alone, 160 people were killed when a rocket landed on the Woolworths department store in Deptford.

Had the rockets been ready earlier, however, the impact on the war may have been very different. General Eisenhower, in his book *Crusade in Europe*, suggests that it would have made the invasion 'exceedingly difficult' and perhaps even impossible. While Winston Churchill, in his history *The Second World War*[54] thinks this something of an exaggeration, he did say that the attack on Peenemünde '… played an important and definite part in the general progress of the war'.

Start of large-scale manufacture was delayed and the fear of subsequent attacks on the site, which obliged the Germans to move their factories deep into the mountains, was tangible proof of success.

Whether contemporary military figures or post-war historians can agree on the ultimate 'success' of the Peenemünde raid is probably not important. What they all agree on is the brilliance of the Master Bomber, Searby, and the bravery of the men under his command. That there is not a formal memorial to these men and their sacrifice is a source of bitterness to those few who survive, and to the families of the dead and missing.

Experience, in wartime, is a commodity often in short supply. Survival rates in Bomber Command have been a feature of many books and discussions, and Ray Raphael's crew, in particular, had the type of experience that was difficult to replace.

Francis Garrett, one of the air gunners, was killed on the eighteenth trip of his second tour. Given a first tour of thirty operations, and a 'one-off' at OTU, Francis had at least forty-nine operations under his belt; Derrick Fielden had similarly flown more than fifty trips, so both men were flying one of the last trips of their second tour, after which no volunteer could be obliged to return for a third. They had come that close to surviving.

In April 1941 Ron Carter, navigator to Ray Raphael in Lancaster LM342, sent a letter to his parents during his voyage from Nova Scotia to England. He wrote: 'I probably shouldn't even mention it, but if anything does happen to me, remember you can count on the fact that I went down fighting.'

Ron did indeed go down fighting, and it seems wrong that he, and those others who died, are now apparently being 'forgotten' for lack of MoD funding. Both the British and the Canadian governments wrote to the parents of the bereaved to promise them that they would not cease in their quest to find the missing men. The letter says: 'You may be assured that if at some future date, it becomes possible to recover your son's remains, he will be moved to a Military Cemetery and his grave given permanent care by the Imperial War Graves Commission (A13).'

Perhaps it is now possible for those remains to be recovered, and perhaps now time too for both governments to honour their commitments to the surviving families these brave men left behind.

Appendix

Supporting Documents

```
EDN/B              TELEGRAM EN CLAIR.                105/18
                   IMPORTANT NOTWT.

TO:- AIR MINISTRY KINGSWAY AIR GROUP OXFORD HEADQUARTERS
     BOMBER COMMAND HEADQUARTERS NO. 5 GROUP RECORDS
     GLOUCESTER RAF BASE SCAMPTON.
FROM:- 44 SQUADRON DUNHOLME LODGE.

RECEIVED A.M.C.S. KINGSWAY 1948 HRS. 18TH AUG. 1943.

A.81 18TH AUG. FOR ATTENTION C.1.ACCIDENTS AND P.4. CAS
AIR MINISTRY FB.
(A) LANCASTER MARK 111 DV. 202 MERLIN XXV111 PO 3539/267
    493 P.I. 6505/325794 SI 6098/325522 SO 6090/325519.
(B) NO. 44 SQUADRON (RHODESIA)
(C) NOT KNWON PRESUMED OVER TARGET NIGHT 17/18TH AUG.
    1943.
(D) (1) J.17338 P/O REGINALD CLIFFORD HARDING (CAN) PILOT
    1379790 SGT THOMAS NEVILLE WESTON F/ENG1127532 T/F/SGT
    LESLIE PRENDERGAST NAV. 1802253 T/SGT LEONARD FRANK
    MC. DERMOTT A/BOM 1213933 T/SGT WILLIAM HENRY QUANCE
    WO/AG 1576142 T/F/SGT STANLEY SHAW ACH/AG R104462 T/F/
    SGT. PETER PYNISKY (CAN) ACH/AG (11) ALL MISSING.
(E) NOT KNOWN.
(F) IFF TR. 1355 CAMERA 1 X 4000 HC 4 SB 150X/ 4 LB 6
    SBC 12 X 30 LB. 4 SBC 16 X 30 LB.
(G) PRESUMED ENEMY ACTION
(H) CAT E MISSING
(J) N.A.
(K) KINFORMED WESTON PRENDERGAST, MC.DERMOTT. QUANCE,
    SHAW, PYNISKY, KINOT. HARDING NEXT OF KIN FATHER
    MR. R.V. HARDING 87. SECOND ST. KIRKLAND LAKE,
    ONTARIO CANADA.

        TIME OF ORIGIN. 1136A

CRASH CIRC. ADVANCE COPY SENT TO P.4. CAS.
P.4. CAS CAN. (2 COPIES)
P.4. CAS (10 COPIES)
```

(A1) Telegram sent from No. 44 Squadron at RAF Dunholme Lodge to Air Ministry Casualty Section, Kingsway, giving details of the loss of Lancaster DV202. *(Author's Collection)*

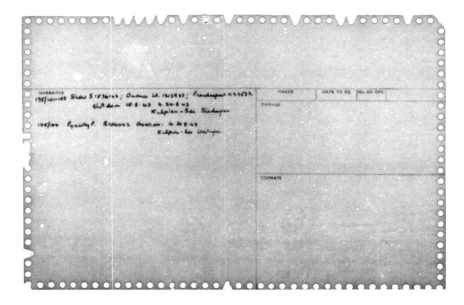

(A2) Loss Card initiated with the report of the loss of DV202. Details of the crew, aircraft, target, squadron, base, bomb load and route were included. As news came through initially from the Totenlistes it would be added to the card, in this case 'Dead' and the Totenliste reference was written next to the names of Prendergast, Quance, Pynisky and Shaw. *(Author's Collection)*

The rear of the Loss Card showing the names and numbers of Shaw, Quance and Prendergast shot down 18.8.43 and buried 24.8.43. at the Kolpiensee sudufer, or south shore. Pynisky is noted as buried on 21.8.43 on the west shore of the lake. *(Author's Collection)*

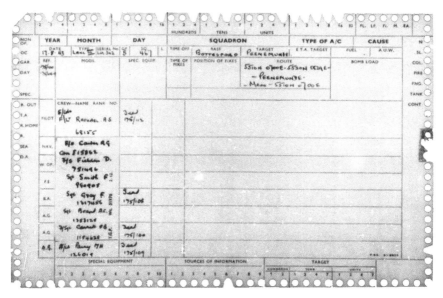

(A3) Similarly the Loss Card for LM342 has been marked up with the word 'Dead' adjacent to the
names of Raphael, Grey, Garrett and Parry. *(Author's Collection)*

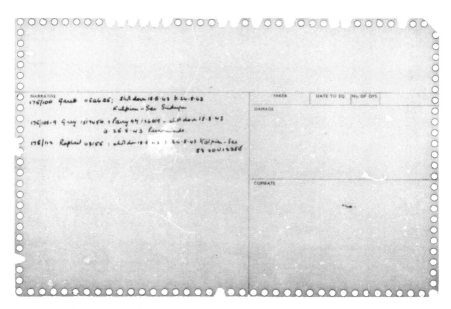

The rear of the Loss Card shows the four airmen as shot down on 18.8.43 with Garrett also being
buried on the south shore of the Kölpien-See on 24.8.43. Grey and Parry are shown as being buried
at Peenemünde on 25.8.43. Raphael is listed as buried at the Kölpien-See on 24.8.43. A map reference
has been added which is erroneous. *(Author's Collection)*

P. 407629/43

Translated extract from Official Death Lists (Totenliste No....175..........)

forwarded by International Red Cross Committee, page ....9.......
(Original filed in P.4 Cas.)

Name	Number	Rank
SHAW S. AIRMAN	1576142	Buried 24.8.43
CHANCE W. "	1213933	" "
PRENDERGAST "	RAF B.64 1127532	" "
X Buried Kolpien-See, South Shore.		
PYNISKY F. Sgt	Can.R.104442	Buried 21.8.43.
REMARKS		Kolpien-See, West Shore

(See also S BCD 624)

..Shot down 13.8.43

O.KOLPIN- SEE, MECKLENBURG, Germany............................ 30/12/43

⊗ R.104462. T/Sgt. PYNISKY.   (*12655) Wt. 21364—1105 200 Pads 8/43 T.S. 700

(A4) As the Totenlistes, or Official Death Lists as they were also known, were received via the Red Cross in Geneva they would be translated, and the names sorted into crew members according to the Air Ministry casualty files. This extract for the DV202 crew members gives the location of the crash as the Kolpin-See, Mecklenburg, which is almost 100 miles from the Kölpien-See where they were actually buried. *(Author's Collection)*

(A5) (The records opposite in German were recovered by the Allies in April and May 1945 from the German administrative headquarter at Meiningen in Thuringia.) German telegram from the commander of Peenemünde Airfield to various administrative centres in Germany including Dulag Luft Oberursel sent on 24.8.43. It refers to the crash of what was believed to be a Halifax bomber, shot down by a night fighter and the burial of six airmen. These were Prendergast, Shaw, Pynisky, Quance, Garrett and one unknown at the place they were found. It goes on to state that the identification tags had been sent to the commander of the airfield at Greifswald for processing. *(Author's Collection)*

Fernschreibstelle

Fernschreibname   Laufende Nr.

Angenommen
Aufgenommen

Datum: 26 : 8 : 43   19......   Befördert: Datum: 19......

um: Uhr   um: Uhr

von: LF/13   an:

durch: durch:

Rolle:

Vermerke: -- QEM --

Fernschreiben
Radiotelegramm   von

+   SSD MKZE 5279 24.8. 2040 DGZ=

AN SSD LGK ROEM ELF, ABT ROEM EINS C, HAMBURG - BL'NESE =

GLTD : SSD DULAG LUFT OBERURSEL,- SSD LGK ROEM ELF,

ABT ROEM EINS C, HAMBURG - BL'NESE,- SSD KDO FL H BER

6/ ROEM ELF, ABT ROEM EINS C, SCHWERIN,-

BETR : SERGEANT TAYLOR, ROY, ERK, NR 1351520,-

VORG: DIESS, FS, V, 21.8.43,-   113922

ERGAENZEND WIRD GEMELDET .: FLUGZEUGMUSTER : HALIFAX,-

KENNZEICHEN: M K,- ZULASSUNGS- NR : NICHT FESTSTELLBAR,-

ABSCHUSZURSACHE: NACHTJAEGER,- BISHER WURDEN DIE LEICHEN

VON 6 BESATZUNGSMITGLIEDERN GEBORGEN, INFOLGE

FORTGESCHRITTENER VERWESUNG KONNTEN NUR DIE

ERKENNUNGSMARKEN GEBORGEN WERDEN, LAUT ERKENNUNGSMARKEN

Lina Drewitz, Berlin SW 61.

HANDELT ES SICH UM: BREDERGAST B G 4, 1127532 C O F, RAF,-

SCHAW, 1576142 C, E, PYNISKYN SGT, , CAN, R 104462,-

QUANCE, 1213933 RAF, GARRETT, 1154625 V NN 1154625 C, E,-

INDENTIFIZIERUNG DER 6, LEICHE NICHT MOEGLICH,

DA ERK,- MARKE NICHT AUFFINDBAR, ,- BEISETZUNG DER TOTEN

MUSZTE AM AUFFINDUNGSORT ERFOLGEN, DIE ERKENNUNGSMARKEN

WURDEN HEUTE AN FLUGPL, KDO GREIFSWALD ZWECKS WEITERLEITUNG

NACH DORT ABGEGEBEN=

FL PL KDO A 34/ ROEM ELF PEENEMUENDE ROEM EINS +

113923

Copy for R.C.A.F.

Extract from German Documents   Crash & P.O.W.

Type of aircraft   HALIFAX

Date and time of crash   18·8·43

Location :-   near   PEENEMÜNDE

Nature of crash :-

Crew :-   6 dead

(1)   PREDEGAST   1127532.

(2)   SHAW   1576142

(3)   PYNISKYN   Sgt: R104462

(4)   QUANCE   1213933

(5)   unidentified   No diss.

(6)   GARRET   1154625   (not a member of this crew)

(7)

Cemetery :-

Other information   Dead buried in place where they were found.

Copies to :-   Signed   Hark. M.R.J. CS

                                    Date.   25·3·47.

      0.95904.

(A6) It had taken several years to sift through and translate the huge amount of documents recovered from Germany. Above is an extract of the translation of the previous telegram – it was not received by the Casualty Section until 25.3.47. It bears the details of the six airmen with the statement that "Dead buried in the place they were found". *(Author's Collection)*

COMITÉ INTERNATIONAL DE LA CROIX-ROUGE

AGENCE CENTRALE DES PRISONNIERS DE GUERRE

Rappeler dans la réponse :

S.Brit.EBav 2828/18-32/ GENÈVE, 3.7.44.

Chèques postaux I. 5527
Téléphone 4 23 03
Téleg. "Intercroixrouge"

Oberkommando der Wehrmacht
Wehrmachtauskunftstelle
M e i n i n g e n .

Betrifft: Gefallene britische Fliegerbesatzungen

- Acting Squadron Leader A.S.RAPHAEL, 68155
- Sgt. V. SMITH, 980905
- Sgt. F. GREY, 1317456
- F/Sgt. D. FIELDEN, 751496
- Sgt. A.C. BRAND, 1353125
- F/Sgt. F.B. GARRETT, 1154625
- Acting F/Lieut. M.H. PARRY, 126019
- Flying Officer R.G. CARTER, J.15862

- Sgt. L.F. McDERMOTT, 1802253
- Temporary Sgt. W.H. QUANCE, 1213933
- Sgt. T.N. WESTON, 1379790
- Pilot Officer L. PRENDERGAST, 155580
- F/Sgt. S. SHAW, 1576142
- F/Sgt. P. Pynisky, R. 104462
- Pilot Officer R.C. HARDING, J. 17338

Bezug: Totenliste 175/100-112.

Diese beiden Flugzeuge wurden am 18.8.43
abgeschossen. Raphael, Grey, Garrett und Parry von der
ersten Besatzung und Quance, Prendergast, Shaw und
Pynisky von der zweiten Besatzung verloren dabei das
Leben. Sie haben die beiden Besatzungen als eine betrachtet,
wahrscheinlich, da das Abschussdatum und die Grablage
überein stimmen. Laut der o.a. Liste wurden Raphael, Garrett,
Quance, Prendergast, Shaw und Pynisky am Kölpinsee,

(A7) On 3 July 1944 at the request of the Air Ministry this follow up letter was sent by the Red Cross in Geneva to the Wehrmachtauskunftstelle or Wehrmacht Information Office at Meiningen requesting further information regarding the crews of DV202 and LM342 and also three reported 'unknown' burials. The reverse of the letter is shown on the following page. *(Author's Collection)*

Mecklenburg, und Grey und Parry in Peenemünde
beigesetzt. In der gleichen Liste meldeten Sie
uns als Grablage von 3 Unbekannten, die am gleichen
Tage gefallen sind, ebenfalls Peenemünde. Handelt
es sich vielleicht bei diesen um Mitglieder der
oben erwähnten Besatzungen?

Wir wären Ihnen dankbar, wenn Sie nach dem
Schicksal und dem Verbleib der als vermisst ge-
meldeten Flieger Smith, Fielden, Brand und Carter
von der ersten Besatzung und Dermott, Weston und
Harding von der zweiten Besatzung nachforschen
würden.

Ferner bitten wir Sie um Auskunft über die
Grabnummern der in Peenemünde und am Kölpinsee
bestatteten Flieger und um Mitteilung, ob irgend-
welche Nachlassgegenstände vorhanden sind.

Für Ihre Bemühungen sprechen wir Ihnen zum
voraus unseren besten Dank aus und zeichnen

mit vorzüglicher Hochachtung

Comité international de la Croix Rouge
Agence centrale des prisonniers de guerre
GENÈVE

(A8) The previous letter shown on page 93 and opposite, prompted this draft letter, above written from Meiningen to Referat IV referring to their own records and requesting information. The draft refers to Pynisky, Shaw, Prendergast, Quance (DV202) Garrett and Raphael (LM342) killed 18.8.43 and buried 28.8.43 at the Kölpien-See Sudufer or south shore and Grey and Parry (LM342) also fallen on 18.8.43 and buried at the Flugplatz or airfield at Peenemünde. Reference is then made to three Unbekannter or unidentified airmen who also fell on 18.8.43. One was recorded as buried at the Liegeplatz or moorings, the second at the west side of the airfield and the third at the Ufer or shore of the airfield, all at Peenemünde.*(Author's Collection)*

(A9) The German KE Record was completed using information from Stan Shaw's identity tag. On the right hand side the word 'Tod', meaning dead, has been underlined. Absturz, meaning crash, has been added. The date of death is indicated by the cross next the date 18.8.43 and 'Grablage' or burial is given as 24.8.43 at the Kölpien-See Sudufer or south shore. The remarks in red ink were added as a result of the Red Cross inquiry letter. *(Author's Collection)*

On the rear of the card it is stated that the information came from the airfield commander at Greifswald, which is where the identity tags had been sent from Peenemünde. The Totenliste details are given as number 101 on list number 175, or 175/101. The details were forwarded to the Red Cross on 21.10.43. There is also a reference to the Red Cross Enquiry letter of 3.7.44. *(Author's Collection)*

(A10) The KE Record for Frank Grey is similar to Stan Shaw's except that the burial details are given as 25.8.43 at the Flugplatz or airfield, Peenemünde. The comments on the reverse of the card indicate the Totenliste reference as 175/108. *(Author's Collection)*

(A11) Squadron Leader Raphael's card gives his burial as simply the Kölpien-See. The additional information in red ink is acknowledged as being 'V Int. R. Kr.', which is a German abbreviation for 'From the International Red Cross'. Raphael's Totenliste reference is 175/112. (*Author's Collection*)

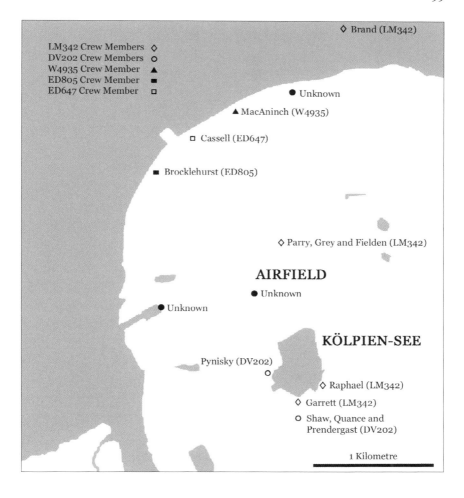

◇ Brand (LM342)

LM342 Crew Members ◇
DV202 Crew Members ○
W4935 Crew Member ▲
ED805 Crew Member ■
ED647 Crew Member ▫

● Unknown

▲ MacAninch (W4935)

▫ Cassell (ED647)

■ Brocklehurst (ED805)

◇ Parry, Grey and Fielden (LM342)

AIRFIELD
● Unknown

● Unknown

KÖLPIEN-SEE

Pynisky (DV202)
○

◇ Raphael (LM342)

◇ Garrett (LM342)

○ Shaw, Quance and
  Prendergast (DV202)

1 Kilometre

(A12) Map showing indicative grave locations based on the German and British records. The location indicated for Brand is the best estimate of where he entered the water. *(Mike McLeod)*

IN REPLY PLEASE QUOTE

No. J19930 (DPC)

Department of National Defence

CANADA

OTTAWA, Ontario,
10 November, 1951.

Mr. Stephen Pynisky,
12 Sutherland Street,
Sydney, N.S.

Dear Mr. Pynisky:

It is with reluctance that after so long an interval,
I must again refer to the loss of your son, Pilot Officer Peter Pynisky.

Through the translation of captured German documents,
it was ascertained that your son's aircraft crashed in the Kolpin See,
Neustrelitz, Province of Mecklenberg, and that Flight Sergeant Shaw,
Sergeant Quance and Pilot Officer Prendergast were buried in the South
Shore, and your son on the West shore of the Kolpin See. No mention is
made of the remaining members of the crew. The Kolpin See is in the Russian occupied Zone of Germany. Unfortunately, it has not been possible
to visit this area to confirm the burial places of the crewmembers listed
in the German documents, and to conduct a search for the burial place of
the unaccounted for crewmembers.

The Imperial War Graves Commission (of which Canada is
a member) are entrusted with the care and maintenance of all the graves
of our fallen and the commemoration of all those who do not have "known"
graves. The Commission has decided that in all cases of this kind, commemoration will be made on General Memorials erected at a number of locations. Each Memorial will be representative of a theatre of operations.
One of these Memorials will be erected at Runnymede, England, and the name
of your son will appear on that Memorial.

You May be assured that if, at some future date, it be-
comes possible to recover your son's remains, he will be moved to a Military
Cemetery and his grave given permanent care by the Imperial War Graves Commission.

..2..

RCAF G32B
215M—2-51 (6700)

(A13) This letter is similar to letters sent to all the airmen who were recorded as being buried by the
Germans at Peenemünde. In this case it is the Canadian government that promise to retrieve the
bodies once access to the area is possible. Since 1990 and the fall of the Berlin Wall the area has been
accessible however the promise appears to have been conveniently forgotten and the bodies still lie
according to the German records 'Buried where they fell'. *(Author's Collection)*

..2..

        I realize that this is an extremely distressing letter and
that there is no manner of conveying such news to you that would not add
to your heartaches, and I am fully aware that nothing I may say will lessen
your great sorrow, but I would like to take this opportunity of expressing
to you and the members of your family my deepest sympathy in the loss of
your gallant son.

                                        Yours sincerely,

                                        (W.R. Gunn)
                                        Wing Commander,
                                        R.C.A.F. Casualties Officer,
                                        for Chief of the Air Staff.

Acknowledgements and Bibliography

'Peenemünde? Where exactly is Peenemünde?'
It was this question, asked in the spring of 2015 by Jackie McLeod, Mike's wife, that started the all-consuming and occasionally frustrating quest to discover the truth about something that happened seven decades ago. Jackie's uncle, Derrick Fielden, had served in the RAF and was lost on the raid to Peenemünde. All the family knew was that he had no known grave. They believed he had been killed in a mid-air collision. And they believed, also, that only two bodies from his aircraft had ever been found.

The first time that Jackie learned that her uncle's body had been found by the Germans and buried on the airfield at Peenemünde was in a letter from Stuart Hadaway of the RAF Air Historical Branch, dated 5 November 2015. Sadly, this was too late for many of his closest relatives. Jackie and Mike's quest quickly became a shared journey with other relatives who also had no idea that their loved-ones' bodies were not 'missing' but rather had been 'forgotten'.

The authors would therefore like to thank the following for their generous help and support in telling the story of the forgotten graves. Indeed, without their enthusiasm, and information and memories about their relatives, this book would not have been possible.

Jackie McLeod – niece to Derrick Fielden
Elaine Towlson, daughter, and **Russell Towlson**, grandson, of Stan Shaw
Peter Garrett – nephew to Francis Garrett
Frank Shern, nephew, and **Matt** and **Ryan Shern**, great nephews, of Frank Grey
Barrie Carter and **Michael Goldstein** – relatives of Ron Carter
Vivienne Stone – niece to Vivian Smith
Nic Raphael – relative of Ray Raphael
Barbara Goldstone – daughter of Tommy Weston
James Quance – grandson of William Quance
Steve Jeffels – nephew to Leslie Prendergast
Wendy Delisle and **Dave** and **Maralyn Reynolds** – for information on Vivian Smith.

The authors would also like to thank Kai Schaake M.A., the archaeologist, and Mick Swindells, Search Dogs United Kingdom, for their continued support, David Fell for his encyclopaedic knowledge of No. 103 Squadron, Dr. Marcel Bradtmöller and Dr. Daniel Winger, Rostock University, Dr. U Fuellhaus, Bund für Umwelt und Naturschutz Deutschland, for permission to access Peenemünde, Mr. D. Weier (Untere Naturschutzbehörde des Landkreises Vorpommern-Greifswald) for permission to access the nature reserve at Peenemünde.. We would also like to thank Steve Darlow of Fighting High for his passion for preserving the memory of Bomber Command and believing this quest to be worthy of wider publication.

Archive Sources
AIR20/7055 – MRES Russian Zone
AIR29/1598 – MRES Berlin Detachment
AIR27/2007 – No. 540 Squadron ORB
AIR27/450 – No. 44 Squadron ORB
AIR27/453 – No. 44 Squadron Appendices
AIR27/645 – No. 75 Squadron ORB
AIR27/1930 – No. 467 Squadron ORB
AIR20/9050 – Casualties
AIR 55/65, Air Ministry, Group Captain E.F. Hawkins, 'Report on Royal Air Force and Dominions Air Forces Missing Research and Enquiry Service 1944–1949'.
AIR2/10031, Air Ministry Casualty Branch, Squadron Leader A.P. LeM Sinkinson, 'Missing Research: Origin and Development', report, 21 April 1948.
MRES AIR20/4040 – Report on the Peenemünde raid by W/C Searby, 10 December 1948.
RAFM B3924 – Peenemünde Burial Schedule
Night Raid Report 404 – Peenemünde
AM File T.24712/48 – Schedule of Burials – Peenemünde Raid.
Service records for Reg Harding, Ron Carter and Peter Pynisky are held by Library and Archives Canada (LAC) in Ottowa.

Other Sources
Flying log book of Derrick Fielden
Flying log book of Francis Garrett
Bottesfordhistory.org.uk
No. 44 Squadron Association
Bomber Command Losses (1943) – W.R. Chorley
Nachtjagd War Diaries – Dr Theo Boiten.

Suggested Further Reading
Missing Believed Killed – Stuart Hadaway
On the Wings of the Morning – RAF Bottesford, 1941–45 – Vincent Holyoak
Operation Crossbow – Bomben auf Peenemünde – Manfred Kanetzki
The Peenemünde Raid – Martin Middlebrook

Endnotes

1 Boyce wrote later: 'On the spur of the moment I decided to go on the raid itself; I suppose because it was something special. I told the Squadron Commander that I would like to go along and could he find me a nice reliable pilot to fly with. I had my flying suit in my car and I drew the rest of the equipment there. I didn't tell the AOC, Bennett, but he probably wouldn't have minded.' Boyce flew with Squadron Leader Ernest Rodley of No. 97 Squadron, although his senior passenger does not feature in the squadron's Operations Record Book.

2 Bowes would subsequently be awarded the DFC for his leadership over Peenemünde and a Bar in early 1944. He survived the war.

3 The Fleet Finch was a dedicated training aircraft, not dissimilar to the DH82 Tiger Moth but with the appearance more of the Avro 504.

4 The official change from observer to navigator came in September 1942, after Prendergast had arrived at No. 25 OTU.

5 John Dering Nettleton was born on 28 June 1917 in Nongoma, Natal Province, South Africa, the grandson of an admiral. Educated at Western Province Preparatory School (WPPS) in Cape Town, Nettleton looked set to follow his grandfather's naval career, serving as a Naval cadet on the General Botha training ship before spending eighteen months in the South African Merchant Marine. He took up civil engineering, before joining the RAF on a short-service commission. Mentioned in Despatches in September 1940, by the summer of 1941 he was a squadron leader and one of the first to fly the Lancaster operationally. In April 1942 he led one of two formations tasked with a deep-penetration raid on the MAN diesel engine factory at Augsburg in Bavaria, in daylight, for which he was awarded the VC for 'valour of the highest order'. Out of his formation of six Lancasters, his was the only aircraft to return.

6 Canadian Ken Brown had flown his first 'second dickey' with Squadron Leader Whitehead, DFC, only a few weeks earlier. Brown, with most of his crew, was posted to No. 617 Squadron for the Dams Raid, having completed only seven operations with No. 44 Squadron.

7 Olding was later commissioned, and shot down on the night of 13/14 May during an attack on Pilsen (Plzeň). He was the only survivor from his crew of seven. Their

Lancaster was the victim of Hauptman Herbert Lutje of 3./NJG1.

8   Pilot Officer Lawrence Pilgrim was later awarded a DFC for his coolness and keenness
     on operations. He survived the war and remained in the RAF on a permanent
     commission.

9   It wasn't that easy. Two aircraft from No. 44 Squadron failed to return: Olding and
     Rail. Olding survived; William Rail, from Vumba, southern Rhodesia, was killed,
     along with all of his crew.

10   Burness transferred from No. 44 Squadron to No. 630 Squadron in November 1943
     and completed his tour. Later commissioned, Burness served as an instructor until
     the end of the war, adding the Air Force Cross to an immediate DFM he earned for an
     eventful trip over Kassel when he was obliged to make three runs over the target and
     release his bombs manually. He died in 1968. John Shorthouse was later promoted to
     squadron leader and appointed flight commander. He was awarded an immediate
     DFC for attacking Mülheim in September 1943. He was listed as wounded in action
     in an Air Ministry Casualty Communiqué in July 1940. After the war he became a
     civilian airline pilot and died in 2007.

11   Dunholme Lodge was constructed as a Class A bomber airfield featuring a 2,000-yard
     main runway and two 1,400-yard secondary runways. It also had hard-surface
     perimeter tracks and hard-standings, and two prefabricated metal hangars (known as
     T2 hangars). Construction was led by renowned building contractor, George Wimpey.

12   Williamson was a regular officer who'd been granted a short service commission in
     August 1936. Among his contemporaries published in the London Gazette are
     Marmaduke Pattle, Mike Beytagh and R.G. Dutton, all notable wartime fighter pilots,
     and Mike Casey and Tom Kirby Green, later murdered as two of 'the fifty' who took
     part in the Great Escape.

13   Frankie Fox flew operationally with No. 75 (NZ) Squadron throughout the war,
     including a tour on Lancasters in 1944 for which he was awarded a very well earned
     and long-overdue DFC as a flight lieutenant. Fox had similarly started his operational
     career as a second pilot. Other notable pilots on the squadron during that time
     include Squadron Leader 'Popeye' Lucas, a charismatic and much-respected bomber
     captain who went on to write about his exploits after the war in his book, *Popeye
     Lucas: Queenstown.* Ray was also a contemporary of Sergeant Ward, VC.

14   Harry Machin went on to fly with No. 12 Squadron and was lost on the night of
     31 August 1943 during an attack on Berlin. He had only recently arrived at No. 12
     Squadron from No. 1656 HCU. He was twenty-one.

15   Robert Craig was a well-known swimmer in his home town of Toronto. Local
     contemporary newspaper reports state that Craig was one of the first Canadian
     graduates of the Commonwealth Air Training Plan to fly in a bomber across the
     Atlantic Ocean (he flew in a formation of eighteen aircraft). A former pupil of
     Franklin Public School and Danforth Technical School, he enlisted in June 1940.
     He is buried in Scottow Cemetery in Norfolk.

     The rest of the crew flying with Ray Raphael that night included the British
     second pilot, Harry Machin, Australian wireless operator Murray McDonald, a New
     Zealand front gunner, Campbell Aitchison, and rear gunner Joseph Godfrey. All were
     sergeants. McDonald, Aitchison and Godfrey were re-crewed with Sergeant John

Parnham, but in sight of completing their tour, were shot down and killed on the night of 12 March 1942 while attacking Kiel.

16   The spare bod flying that night was an Australian, James Grimwade.

17   Notification of a Distinguished Flying Medal for Geoff Appleyard appeared in the London Gazette on 31 July 1942, although contemporary pictures of the pilot show him wearing the ribbon of the DFM before his death. He was awarded the DFM on 17 July for his part on an attack on Danzig in exceptionally poor weather conditions. His observer, Joe Darvill, also received the DFM. The raid on Danzig was Appleyard's seventeenth operation.

18   Tony Ingram had originally joined No. 103 Squadron in 1937, flying Hawker Hinds, Battles and then Wellingtons. He'd fought in the Battle of France, winning the DFC before transferring to a Polish bomber training unit on his arrival back in the UK. Returning to No. 103 Squadron, he was shot down on the night of 21 September 1941, just a few short weeks after his aborted operation with Garrett. He served in the RAF post-war, and later became a journalist and photographer.

19   Signing Francis's log book at No. 29 OTU was Wing Commander Freddie Rainsford, recently returned from the Middle East under something of a cloud after the squadron he commanded almost mutinied owing to their operational conditions. 'Turkey' Rainsford was born in 1909 in Castlebar, County Mayo, where his father was stationed as a member of the Royal Irish Constabulary. Rainsford was educated in Belfast. Rejected by the Royal Navy, he emigrated to Kenya as a pupil farmer, but returned to Belfast following the Depression to enrol at Queen's University to study agriculture. Learning to fly, he was commissioned into the RAF in 1936 and began life instructing before being posted to North Africa and taking command of No. 148 Squadron. Although exhausted by his experience in the desert, he recovered to take command of No. 115 Squadron flying Lancasters and was awarded the DFC. Surviving the war, he played a key role in the Berlin Airlift, for which he was recognised with the CBE. He died in 1999.

20   The OC No. 1660 CU at this time was Wing Commander Russell Oxley, DSO, DFC, OBE, awarded the DSO in April 1942 for leading a daring combined operations attack on Vaagso. Oxley attacked at a height of only 100 feet, his aircraft being hit several times. The citation for his DSO made reference to his inspiring leadership, skill and courage throughout.

21   One of Frank's poems, 'The Blind Collier', survives.

22   Six Wellingtons were lost that night including three from No. 166 Squadron, and one each from No. 27 OTU, No. 199 Squadron, and No. 426 Squadron. There were only two survivors, both from the No. 199 Squadron Wellington X (HZ582) flown by Sergeant H.W. Austin. The two were Sergeant D.R. Keavers, RAAF, and Sergeant J.P.E. Last. A further Wellington was hit, and the pilot bailed out, leaving the four remaining crew to fly the damaged bomber home. The air bomber, who had assumed flying duties, was awarded the Conspicuous Gallantry Medal. He later qualified as a pilot in earnest and saw out the war with No. 158 Squadron.

23   The article appeared in the *Daily Sketch* dated 25 May 1943.

24   Colin Wallace completed his tour and was awarded the DFM, the citation making mention of a difficult raid on Hannover during which he was attacked by a night

fighter and two of his crew were wounded. Messenger was commissioned and posted as missing while serving with No. 463 Squadron in December 1943. He was twenty-four years old.

25   Ambrose (service number 40040) was a pre-war regular who had joined the RAAF at Point Cook in July 1936. His contemporaries in gaining a short service commission with the RAF included Bob Bungey (service number 40042), a well-respected fighter pilot, Les Clisby (service number 40043), another well-known fighter ace in the early Battle of France in 1940, and Allan 'Tup' Farrington (40046), who found fame in the Battles of Greece and in the Middle East, before being killed as a Pathfinder with No. 582 Squadron. Another contemporary was Arthur Hubbard (40050), who went on to become the founding officer commanding No. 460 Squadron.

        Don MacKenzie's older brother, Angus, was lost without trace while serving with No. 35 Squadron.

26   'Chucky' Snell was later commissioned and went on to serve with Nos 97 and 635 Squadrons, Pathfinder Force.

27   Ransom was later commissioned and flew with No. 83 Squadron Pathfinder Force. He was killed in action on the night of 20 January 1944.

28   The pilot that night was Pilot Officer James Carrington, RAAF, a 25-year-old from New South Wales. Five of the crew were killed. The air gunner, who survived, was badly injured and was repatriated in early 1945. Derrick Fielden's log book erroneously records flights in W5003 in August, after the aircraft had gone missing. He had presumably confused two aircraft with the same code and designated letter. It shows how even contemporary documents can be misleading and even wrong.

29   Parry, an officer of the RAF Volunteer Reserve, was an old boy of William Hulme Grammar School in Manchester.

30   H2S was given the codename 'Y'. Set operators, called second navigators or nav IIs, were often retrained air bombers. Every member of a Pathfinder crew was trained to undertake at least two duties. Flight engineers, for example, might double as bomb-aimers, which is why in some PFF squadron Operation Record Books (ORBs) an air bomber is not always listed in the crew.

31   Wing Commander John White, a regular Air Force officer, was awarded the DFC for his part in the success of the Peenemünde raid and for 'powers of skill and leadership that have set an outstanding example to other members of his squadron'. Sadly, he did not live long to enjoy it, being lost on a trip to Berlin in November 1943 while conducting his forty-third operation with No. 156 Squadron. He was twenty-eight.

32   Audrey Cooke, from Wichita Falls, had tried to join the US Army Air Corps but been rejected on account of a club foot.

33   The Holmes-A-Court name originated in 1833 with the marriage of William Ashe a Court and Elizabeth Holmes. William later became Lord Heytesbury. Death duties and unwise investments led to the sale of the family estate, prompting many of the family to emigrate to Canada, South Africa and Australia. Walter was later commissioned and killed on the night of 2 January 1944. He was only twenty years of age.

34   Reginald Ash was later commissioned and awarded the DFC. His gunner, 'Spud' Murphy, was also awarded the DFM.

35   Forbes was awarded the DFC at the end of his tour, by which time he had been

promoted to flight lieutenant. The citation makes specific mention of his persistence and determination during the attack on Peenemünde.

36   George Tillotson was from Box Hill, Victoria. Later commissioned, he regularly flew Lancaster P-Pots, adorned with a flying pot and the motto, 'Thermo Excreta!'

37   Of the 457 photographs examined after the raid, 171 of those that showed ground detail were plotted within three miles of the target. In the post-raid report, the author suggests that it is probable that nearly all the aircraft bombed within three miles and the majority within one mile of the aiming point. The smokescreen made an exact assessment impossible.

38   Lady Margaret Ampthill was an English courtier and wife of the former governor of Madras, Oliver Russell, the 2nd Baron Ampthill. In the First World War she was honoured for her work with the Red Cross, a service she continued into the 1940s. She was best known as a favourite of Queen Mary, for whom she served as a lady-in-waiting.

39   Later Wing Commander W.R. Gunn, MBE, RCAF.

40   A comment has been added at the bottom of the draft and appended by the Allies on 23 May 1945 that no reply had been received.

41   At the end of the war, more than 79,000 US Servicemen were unaccounted for, including those buried with honour as unknowns, officially buried at sea, lost at sea, and missing in action. Since then, more than 7,000 have been identified/recovered. The Army-led programme was a worldwide endeavour employing around 13,000 personnel and costing more than $160 million in wartime dollars.

42   The use of advertising may have been at the personal behest of 'Butch' Harris himself. In a letter to the AMP dated 11 February 1946, Harris writes: 'Just met a Dutchman and, I understand, a leading "resistancer". He informs me that the Americans are tracing a lot of their missing airmen's graves and obtaining a great deal of information about others by wholesale advertising in national and local press organs. He says we do none of this and asks why. I told him we had search parties out but he said so do the Americans and that is not enough. I asked for any instance to quote. He replied that in the village of Nunspeet, Gelderland, there are about eight graves of unknowns. No one has been to enquire except the yanks. No RAF, he says.'

43   Hawkins' 'happy flair' may have been a result of his age and experience. A group captain in the RAFVR, Eustace Hawkins had in fact been commissioned 2nd Lieutenant upon the outbreak of the First World War into the Army Service Corps, and by 1918 was a lieutenant colonel with the DSO, having also been Mentioned in Despatches. He was a good thirty years senior to the men under his command.

44   AM File T.24712/48.

45   An aerial photo from 1953 shows much of the infrastructure intact and the buildings still being dismantled by hand for their materials, rather than being 'blown up'.

46   Drew's mother informed her local newspaper, the *Woking News* and *Mail*, that her son was missing and of rumours that he had survived and been taken prisoner. Sadly it was not the case. Spoden ended the war with twenty-five victories, all but one at night. He went on to become a peacetime airline pilot and wrote about his experiences in his book, *Enemy in the Dark*.

47   'Brock' Brocklehurst is remembered on the Holmfirth Memorial near Huddersfield.

48   For the sake of historical completeness, there is one further casualty from the

Peenemünde Raid, notified by the Germans as being buried in the area, that is still waiting to be recovered. Sergeant Robert Lewis was the English flight engineer in the crew of an experienced and long-serving Canadian pilot, Flight Lieutenant Gordon Fanson of No. 428 (Ghost) Squadron RCAF. Lewis had ten trips under his belt; his skipper was flying his twentieth. Their Halifax (DK230) had taken off shortly after 21.00hrs from Middleton St George and was thought to be the twenty-second aircraft to be shot down. The bodies of six of the men were recovered from various cemeteries and subsequently buried in a Commonwealth war grave in Berlin. The body of Robert Lewis was buried at Koos Island, five miles to the north of Greifswald. Attempts to recover his remains by No. 4 MREU were unsuccessful; while the island is small, it has a coastline of around four miles. The search was further complicated by the use of Koos Island as a practice bombing range by the Luftwaffe, leading the searchers to assume that his body may no longer be there. There was the added complication of drifting sands and pressure of time. They dug the only likely looking place but without success. As such, the search was abandoned, and Robert's name is recorded on the memorial to the missing. Local geographers, however, insist the area is not prone to drifting sands, and aerial photographs show minimum damage after 1943. There is a good chance, therefore, that his remains could still be found.

49 Alfred Peverell Le Mesurier Sinkinson, later wing commander, OBE.

50 There are 7,594 Commonwealth servicemen of the Second World War buried or commemorated in the Reichswald Forest War Cemetery. Some 176 of the burials are unidentified. There are around half that number (3,330) Commonwealth servicemen of the Second World War buried or commemorated at Rheinberg War Cemetery, the majority of them airmen. A total of 158 of the burials are unidentified.

51 Frank Grey and Vivian Smith are remembered on the same local memorial.

52 A copy of this page hangs in the RAF Club beneath a dramatic painting of the attack by Frank Wootton.

53 Volume II – Endeavour.

54 Volume V – Closing the Ring.

Index